ḤASIDISM

Popular Judaica Library
General Editor: Raphael Posner

ḤASIDISM

Edited by Aryeh Rubinstein

KETER BOOKS
Jerusalem

P.O. Box 7145, Jerusalem, Israel

Catalog Number 25112
ISBN 0-7065-1456-4

Printed and bound by Keterpress Enterprises, Jerusalem
Printed in Israel

CONTENTS

INTRODUCTION

The very nature of Judaism, as it had developed by the beginning of the Common Era, was such that it carried within it the seeds of sectarianism. Judaism was an organic growth and no formal creed of belief had been created. Indeed, talmudic Judaism comprises an astonishingly wide array of beliefs and views. *Halakhah* lives together with *aggadah*; national particularism is taught side by side with universalism; some passages indicate a theocentric view of life while others are downright humanistic; certain authorities favored asceticism while others deprecated it; there are rabbis who stressed the cultic and ritual aspects of Judaism, and there are others for whom the social teachings of Judaism seem to be of paramount importance. All these views are within the rabbinic tradition and, as long as their advocates did not negate any of the few basic teachings and remained within the relatively wide framework of *halakhah*, are perfectly legitimate.

It is only natural, therefore, that groups should develop which would stress one particular teaching as their main doctrine. And in fact throughout the ages many such groups have arisen, only to disappear. Some of them asserted their distinctive stand, but ultimately sank back into the general body of Judaism. Others became so sectarian as to write themselves out of Judaism, either as new religions or as adjuncts to other religions.

The outstanding example of a doctrine that has at once maintained its individuality and has remained within the Jewish pale is Ḥasidism. The sheer vitality with which it started, and the relatively short time it took to become a major ingredient in European Jewry indicate the real need it must have filled. Even if there was a period of relative relapse after Ḥasidism's initial rise, it seems to have been able to renew itself and today is, if anything, on the rise and, amazingly enough, is making a strong appeal to disillusioned modern youth.

Perhaps the strength of Ḥasidism is the fact that it deals with the human being and is, therefore, a very real teaching. It seems to understand the needs of the person as opposed to the needs of the law or of theology. Menaḥem Mendel of Kotsk is reported to have explained the Ḥasid's apparent disregard for the strict statutory times of prayer by saying that "in Kotsk we have a soul, not a clock." If we may take this *bon mot* further, perhaps we could say that Ḥasidism's main teaching is that "we have a soul, not a book." It could be that it is that very "humanity" which makes Ḥasidism so appealing, particularly in this age of alienation.

Be that as it may, there is no doubt that Ḥasidism succeeded. Notwithstanding the original opposition to it, and some of its own early excesses, Ḥasidism has maintained its own individuality while remaining firmly set within traditional Judaism. This fact alone makes it a subject worth studying, quite apart from the insights that we may gain from its study. This book does not purport to be a full history of Ḥasidism nor an exhaustive account of its doctrines. It does hope to give the reader a taste of Ḥasidism – the flavor, however faint, of the movement which swept Eastern Europe and which may have something to say even today. Its doctrine of joy and *devekut* do so much to make everybody feel that he is somebody. Its teaching that even the most lowly of men is able to communicate with the Almighty, and that all of us have what God desires, is perhaps one of the most comforting ideas a person can contemplate.

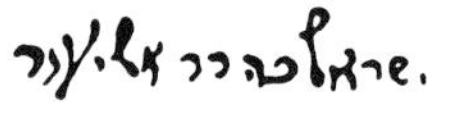

The signature of Israel ben Eliezer Ba'al Shem Tov, the founder of modern Ḥasidism.

1. IN THE WAKE OF SHABBETAI ẒEVI

Even if Ḥasidism had passed into the limbo of history, this pietist-mystical-revivalist movement would be of intense interest to the student of Judaism. Apart from the tremendous impact it has had on Jewish life, Ḥasidism has also influenced modern Christian theology. But Ḥasidism is not only still alive today, it is even experiencing a resurgence that few would have predicted even 50 years ago.

Some Questions About Ḥasidism

Ḥasidism has been described as "the rebellion of the half-illiterate rural Jew against the supremacy of the learned urban Jew." Like many thumb-nail characterizations, however, this is something of an over-simplification of a problem which students of Ḥasidism are still debating. What is the essence of Ḥasidism – was it primarily a religious movement or a social one? What relation did it bear to the messianic movement of Shabbetai Ẓevi, the failure of which had left a gaping wound in the soul of Polish Jewry? Why did the movement come into being when it did?

There are no easy answers to these questions.

About the Name

But first a word about the name. In rabbinic literature the term *ḥasidim* (singular, *ḥasid*) is used to designate pious Jews who maintained a higher standard than most in observing the religious and moral commandments. Although the image of the *ḥasid* was not identical at all times and in all circles, what was common to all religious types to whom the name was applied was a divergence from conventional behavior and the normal standard. Thus the early *ḥasidim* (*ḥasidim ha-rishonim*) referred to in the Mishnah would wait an hour before praying in order to direct their hearts to God. Later the term was applied to persons who evinced ideal and exemplary behavior in some sphere of life. In the Ethics of the Fathers, for example, he who says "what is mine is yours and what is yours is yours" is called a *ḥasid*, and so is "he whom it is hard to provoke and easy to pacify." In medieval Germany a movement emerged known as Ḥasidei Ashkenaz, whose adherents assumed religious duties more severe than the accepted ones. They demanded of themselves the utmost purification of soul and thought and scrupulous observance even of minor precepts.

Bleak Times in Poland

The movement we are concerned with in these pages, however, had its beginnings in the regions of Podolia and Volhynia in southeast Poland in the 1730s and 1740s with the appearance of individuals and small groups of pietists who called themselves Ḥasidim. These were bleak times – even bleaker than usual – for Polish Jewry. The Cossack revolt and massacres under Chmielnicki in 1648-49, the Tatar incursions from Crimea, and the subsequent war with Moscow combined with the Swedish war to bring on the Jews of Poland-Lithuania three decades of bloodshed, destruction and suffering. Thousands were killed,

The *bet ha-midrash* of the Ba'al Shem Tov in Medzibezh, Podolia, on a postage stamp issued by the Israel Post Office in 1960 to commemorate the bicentenary of his death.

thousands were forced to embrace Christianity, and thousands fled westward. The institutions and activities of the Jewish communities lost their dynamism; inertia set in. Much that had been full of imminent promise of development before the disasters now tended to petrify. Then, before they had recovered from these blows, the Jewish communities were beset by a new one: the raids and massacres by the Haidamacks, paramilitary bands consisting mainly of peasant serfs turned brigands, who found the Jews a convenient and defenseless target, and one that could be attacked with the blessing of the Russian Orthodox priests. "Is there no end to this bitter exile?" cried a contemporary rabbi.

In the social and economic decline that followed, the intellectual level of the Jewish masses sank lower and lower. Talmudic learning, formerly widespread, now became the possession of a narrow circle of scholars, while the lower classes stagnated in ignorance and superstition.

The Rabbis Denounced

This dichotemy between the leadership and the people was one of the main themes of the first Ḥasidic book, *Toledot Ya'akov Yosef* (1780), by Rabbi Jacob Joseph of Polonnoye. Its scathing denunciation of the aloofness and arrogance of some of the rabbis and scholars adds another dimension to the background out of which Ḥasidism developed. Rabbi Jacob Joseph found that pride and vanity were very common among the learned. Their sermons, which should have shown the people the path they should follow, were mainly used to display their brilliance. Too many scholars were overly fond of money, a sin which led them to flatter the rich. They permitted the members of the ruling class to act as it pleased so long as their own positions were secure. They felt little obligation towards the people, towards whom their attitude was often one of contempt. All this brought about the condition of *perud*, radical separation between the learned class and the people, and this, Rabbi Jacob Joseph considered the greatest tragedy of his age.

Messianic Fervor Persists

But even more important than the social-communal crisis as a factor that paved the way for the rise of Ḥasidism was the religious crisis: the tense messianic fervor that persisted long after the bankruptcy of Shabbateanism. Shabbetai Ẓevi (1627-76) had aroused feverish messianic expectations among Jewish communities in Turkey, Italy and Poland, after proclaiming himself as the Messiah in May 1665, while on a visit to Palestine. In Smyrna, Turkey, Shabbetai Ẓevi pronounced the Ineffable Name, decreed the abolition of the fast of the Tenth of Tevet, and is said to have promised to free women from the "curse of Eve." On the eve of Passover in 1666 he sacrificed a Passover lamb and roasted it with its fat, inducing his companions to eat this forbidden food and reciting over it the blessing, "He who permits the forbidden." Many of his followers sold their houses and other property to provide themselves with money for the journey to the Holy Land; others made no such preparations, being convinced that they would be transported on clouds. As the fasts of the 17th of Tammuz and the Ninth of Av approached, he not only proclaimed the fasts abolished but introduced new festivals in their stead. The 17th of Tammuz became the "day of the revival of Shabbetai Ẓevi's spirit" and the Ninth of Av the festival of his birthday. Before long, the Turkish authorities became alarmed by Shabbetai Ẓevi's messianic pretensions and activities, and they gave him the choice of being put to death immediately or converting to Islam. He chose the latter alternative.

Shabbetai Ẓevi's Apostasy

Although his apostasy produced a profound shock in Jewry, it did not bring the movement to an abrupt end. Rather than admit that their redeemer was an imposter, many of Shabbetai Ẓevi's followers clung to their belief and sought an explanation of what had happened. That so many refused to give up their faith in Shabbetai Ẓevi even now only shows how deeply rooted the movement was.

Nathan of Gaza

Nathan of Gaza, Shabbetai Ẓevi's "prophet," proved equal to

the new challenge. He came up with a theological explanation of the master's apostasy. This, he argued, was actually the fulfillment of a mission to lift up the holy sparks (see page 20) which were dispersed even among the gentiles and concentrated now in Islam. Only the Messiah could redeem these sparks: he was acting like a spy sent into the enemy camp. By placing the paradox of an apostate Messiah, a tragic but still legitimate redeemer, at the center of the new, developing Shabbatean theology, Nathan laid the foundations for the ideology of the believers for the next 100 years.

Roman Vishniac's picture of an elderly Ḥasid, taken in Cracow in 1938.

6

Caricature of Polish Ḥasidic couple. After L. Hollaenderski *Les Israelites de Pologne*, 1846.

Ten years after his conversion, Shabbetai Ẓevi died quite suddenly, on the Day of Atonement, at the age of 50. But even with his death Shabbateanism did not come to an end. Shabbatean groups continued to be active, and various prophets and claimants to the succession appeared. Many believers proclaimed 1706 as the year of Shabbetai Ẓevi's second advent, and the hundreds of Jews who emigrated to the Land of Israel with Rabbi Judah Ḥasid in 1700 probably were Shabbateans who intended there to await the arrival of the Messiah. And it is not without significance that the regions where Ḥasidism made its first appearance – Podolia and Volhynia – were those where Shabbateanism had found its strongest following.

Secret Rituals

One of Judah Ḥasid's collaborators was Ḥayyim Malakh, who propagated the teachings of Nathan of Gaza among the rabbis of Poland. Malakh later became a spokesman for a radical branch of Shabbateanism, and he spread the gospel of secret antinomianism in Podolia, where he found fertile ground, especially in the smaller communities. The antinomian slogan propagated by the radical wing was that "the nullification of the Torah is its true fulfillment." Like the grain that dies in the earth, it was said, the deeds of man must become in some way "rotten" in order to bring forth the fruit of redemption. Some radical groups, especially in Podolia, performed secret rituals. The eating of forbidden fat (*ḥelev*) or severe transgressions of sexual prohibitions were initiation rites. Not surprisingly, these doctrines and practices alarmed the rabbinic authorities, who considered the children of these sectarians as *mamzerim*, i.e., barred from admission to the Jewish fold.

Shabbateans Go Underground

On the other hand, there is evidence that not a few of the most influential moral preachers and authors of an ethical, ascetic bent were secretly moderate Shabbateans. Even the famous talmudic scholar, Rabbi Jonathan Eybeschuetz (c. 1690-1764) was suspected of Shabbatean leanings and a great uproar ensued, engulfing rabbinic circles in Germany, Austria and Poland in a heated controversy. The Orthodox were deeply shocked by the possibility that an outstanding rabbi might have leanings towards heretical ideas, and they became more apprehensive than ever regarding the entrenchment of the Shabbateans in many communities. The atmosphere of persecution that prevailed, from about 1725 led the remaining Shabbateans to go completely underground for the next 30 years, especially in Poland.

Where Ḥasidism Differed

The circles in Poland known as *ḥasidim* before the advent of the Ba'al Shem Tov, which practiced extreme forms of ascetic piety, contained a strong element of Shabbateanism. Indeed, Gershom Scholem sees Shabbateanism and Ḥasidism as successive stages in the development of Jewish mysticism. Like Shabbateanism, early Ḥasidism was based largely on Kabbalism, particularly on "practical" Kabbalism. But it differed from its predecessors in that it "neutralized" their messianic element. It was an attempt "to preserve those elements of Kabbalism which were capable of evoking a popular response, but stripped of their Messianic flavor." Scholem does not suggest that Ḥasidism dropped the messianic hope; all that he says is that it did not make this the focus of religious life and thought.

Individual Salvation Comes First

Preoccupation with messianism was replaced by emphasis on the personal: it is this that constitutes the originality of Ḥasidism as against the earlier trends in Jewish mysticism. The salvation of the soul of the individual must precede the redemption of the world. Israel Ba'al Shem Tov, the founder of Ḥasidism, forbade (despite the Kabbalistic terminology he frequently employed) any attempt at magical activity designed to hasten the "End of Days." His attitude is clearly seen in a letter to his brother-in-law, Abraham Gershon, in 1751, in which he describes a conversation he had with the Messiah during a spiritual ascent on Rosh Ha-Shanah, 1747: "I asked the Messiah, 'When will you come, master,' and he answered me, 'When your learning will be made known and revealed to the world and its source will spread, and all can recite *yiḥudim* and experience spiritual ascent as you can . . . .' " This he understood to mean that the advent of the

Another of Roman Vishniac's photographs of Ḥasidic life in pre-war Poland.

Messiah was still a long way off: "And I was astonished and deeply grieved by this, and wondered when this would come to pass." Though expressing his deep messianic faith and strong messianic longings, this attitude is far removed from the mystical messianism of Shabbetai Ẓevi that had proved so destructive shortly before.

2. BRINGING HEAVEN DOWN TO EARTH

The Master of the Good Name

Israel Ba'al Shem Tov, Ḥasidism's first teacher and exemplary saint, was born around 1700 in Okop, a small town in Podolia, to poor and elderly parents in the hard times just described. (Ba'al Shem Tov means "the Master of the Good Name," an appellation later bestowed on Israel because of his purported power to perform miraculous cures and feats by invoking the name of God. He is also known as the "Besht," an acronym formed from the initial letters of Ba'al Shem Tov.) Orphaned as a child, he was educated by the community, of which his father Eliezer had been an honored member. But he often escaped from the dark *ḥeder* to seek solitude in the woods. At the age of 12 he became a helper to a schoolmaster, gathering the children from their homes in the morning and taking them back in the evening. On the way he taught them the synagogue hymns, which they sang with such enthusiasm that they penetrated the heavens. A jealous Satan thereupon assumed the shape of a werewolf, and put the children to flight. Fearing for their children's lives, their mothers refused to send them to school the next day, but Israel, remembering his father's last words – that he should fear no one but God – begged for another chance. And when the werewolf appeared a second time, he routed him with a club.

Alone in the Mountains

When he was 14, Israel became a *shammash* (beadle) at the *bet midrash*. He gained a reputation for laziness by dozing about the building all day long. But in the stillness of the night, unobserved, he pored over the *Zohar*. According to tradition, in his twenties, Israel went into isolation in the Carpathian Mountains in preparation for his future tasks, accompanied by his wife, Hannah. Their life was one of great privation; for several years he eked out a living by digging lime, which his wife sold in town. But here he learned the language of the beasts and the birds, of the plants and trees. From the peasant women he learned the healing properties of grasses and herbs. He learned to cure the

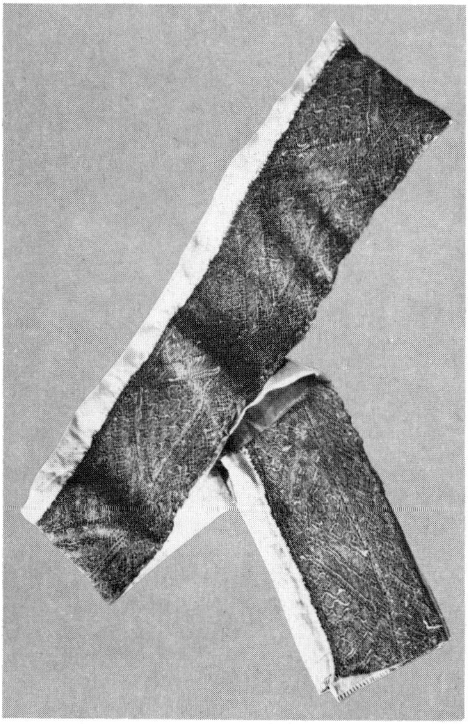

Atarah (neckpiece) of a *tallit* believed to have belonged to the Ba'al Shem Tov, preserved by a descendant of Reb Naḥman of Bratslav.

sick, to drive out evil spirits and to write amulets.

The Besht Acquires Followers

In the mid-1730s – Ḥasidic tradition fixes it on his 36th birthday – Israel revealed himself as a healer and leader. The circle of his followers and admirers widened rapidly. Many were drawn by his magnetism and widespread reports of his miracles, and several groups of Ḥasidim which had formed earlier came under his influence and accepted his leadership to a greater or lesser degree. Tradition hints that some of the members of these Ḥasidic circles were at first repelled by the Ba'al Shem Tov's activity as miracle healer, although he himself was apparently proud of this work.

Painting by the Australian artist Chaim (Hyman) Gorr (1951) of Ḥasidim immersed in prayer; their approach to God is the ecstatic and mystical one of the Ba'al Shem Tov.

The Ba'al Shem Tov was addicted to his pipe and the smoking of a pipe later became a kind of ritual among the early Ḥasidic rabbis and was a target of constant ridicule by opponents of the sect.

Erez Israel

The Ba'al Shem Tov for many years planned to go to Palestine, and once he actually set out on the journey but felt impelled to return. Nine years before his death he wrote to his brother-in-law, Abraham Gershon of Kutow, "God knows that I do not despair of traveling to Ereẓ Israel; however, the time is not right." The Besht's unfulfilled desire became an aim for his followers and in succeeding generations, large organized groups of Ḥasidim made their way to the Holy Land, and made important contributions to the resettlement of the country.

Healing and Magic

The Ba'al Shem Tov undertook journeys to expel demons and evil spirits, and to win influence. In eulogistic folktales, in the tradition handed down by his pupils, and also in writings hostile to him, the interdependence of his healing work and the charisma of his leadership is clearly apparent. Later Ḥasidic tradition, however, tried to depreciate the importance of these healing and magical practices. In tales about him as well as through his teachings, the Ba'al Shem Tov's great personal charm, remarkable magnetism and ecstatic personality are revealed.

Legends About the Besht

Composed even during his lifetime, the legends about the Ba'al Shem Tov's miracles became an integral part of the Ḥasidic atmosphere; they both increased his followers' admiration for him and antagonized his opponents. They have also distorted the Besht's historical character. Disciples who had come in contact with him were among the first to assert his supernatural qualities, but even people who were not among his close associates also spoke of his charismatic personality. There thus developed a literature of *shevaḥim* ("praises"), the first anthology of such legends being *Shivḥei ha-Besht*, published in 1814. It contains about 230 stories with a variety of motifs. They portray the Ba'al Shem Tov as healing the sick, exorcising demons, and resuscitating a child. By opening the *Zohar* the Besht is able to tell a

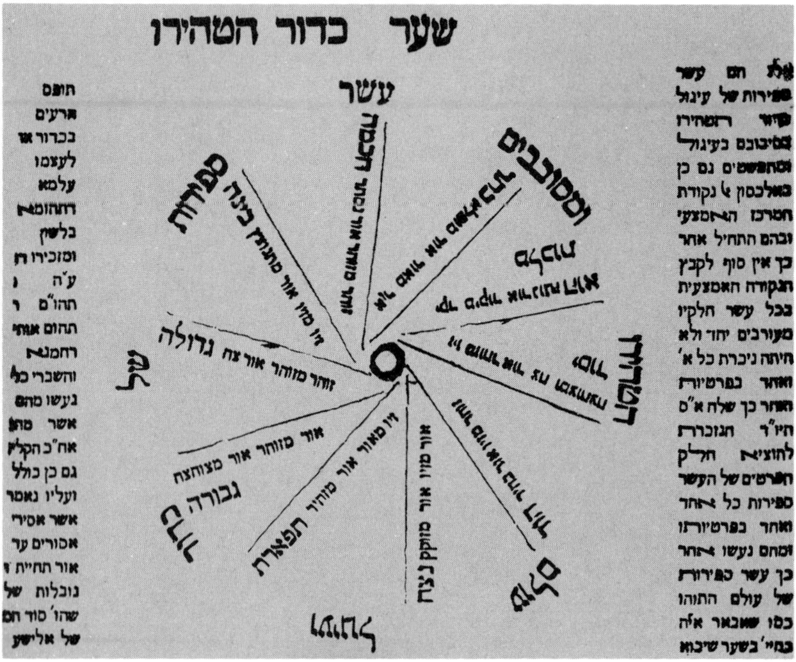

Graphic representation of the kabbalistic doctrine of the ten *sefirot* (emanations) of God from *Emek Hamelekh* by Naftali Herz ben Jacob Elḥanan, Amsterdam, 1648.

Elijah Appears

distraught father that his son will soon return from a business trip from which he was overdue. Once, when the Besht is pulling a wagon of flour home for the baking of *mazzot* for Passover (his horse having died on the way) and, exhausted, cries aloud to God, the Prophet Elijah appears to him and assures him that all will be well. There are some striking parallels to gospel mythology, such as the story that relates that although the Besht was not intimate with his wife for 14 years his son Hershele was born during this time by the word of God. Some of the stories tell that the Ba'al Shem Tov could detect the Angel of Death hovering about a person. The following is one of these, and it will also serve as an example of the legends as a whole:

> A tax farmer who had bad luck came to the Besht. The Besht saw the Angel of Death dancing behind him. He strongly warned him to repent of his sins: "Why do you pursue the affairs of this world? It would be better for you to repent and correct your ways."
>
> The man suspected that the Besht wanted some money. He offered him some coins, but the Besht refused to take them. When the tax farmer left, the Besht said "The fool, He will die today or tomorrow, and he worries about his luck."
>
> His brother-in-law, the rabbi, our teacher, Rabbi Gershon, scolded him and said: "Why did you speak evil against a Jew?"
>
> He answered him: "What can I do about it if you are blind and did not see the Angel of Death following behind him?"
>
> At that time, the brother-in-law of the Besht, our rabbi and teacher, Jacob, was a widower, and he went on a journey to be remarried. He was accompanied by this same tax farmer, since both of them had to go the same way.
>
> They slept overnight at an inn. The tax farmer ordered a fine dinner. Rabbi Jacob did not want to eat meat, and they gave him dairy food at the end of the table. The tax farmer mocked him. Afterwards they went to sleep. During the night the tax farmer awoke with a severe headache and he cried

out. He asked that someone say the rite of confession with him.

Rabbi Jacob said the prayer and the tax farmer recited the confession after him. In a little while he was dead.

Then Rabbi Jacob returned home to tell that indeed we are blind.

Despite its imaginary legendary character, *Shivḥei ha-Besht* includes undoubtedly reliable traditions, and many of the historical events recalled are confirmed in non-Ḥasidic sources. But even Ḥasidim had reservations about the work, especially the

"Ḥasidic Dance," woodcut by Jakob Steinhardt (1961).

strange stories that aroused the scorn of the Mitnaggedim and Maskilim, who used it as a weapon in their war against Ḥasidism.

Ecstatic Prayer

Prayer was the Ba'al Shem Tov's main ecstatic and mystic approach to God; intellectual study and learning took a secondary place. In especially exciting moments he reached a state of mystical exaltation – *aliyyat neshamah* – of which he gave detailed descriptions. Future events and past personalities, both good and evil were shown to him in dreams. But many of his dreams and visions are related to the actual problems and sufferings of the Jews in his generation. In traditional tales he is portrayed as engaged in conversation, and in meeting with people, including women, individually or in small groups. He is never described as preaching in a synagogue. The Besht's teachings do not reveal any talmudic scholarship, and his opponents criticized him for lacking such erudition and for his preoccupation with healing, writing amulets and his conversing with simple men. David of Makow (died 1814), one of the most noted polemicists against early Ḥasidism, considered him a quack who told fortunes for monetary compensation.

Importance of Joy

One of the Besht's principal teachings was that prayer is acceptable to God only if it flows from a joyous heart. In fact, he maintained, devotional joy is the proper attitude of the Jew every moment of his life, and not during prayer alone. The Ba'al Shem Tov exemplified these views through his own attitude to life and his own mode of prayer. His admirers told especially of the light and fire that seemed to emanate from him, and of the fiery way in which he recited his prayers. Even more than his teachings, Israel's idealized personality became the inspiration for the life and aspirations of the Ḥasidim down to the present day.

The Ba'al Shem Tov was aware of his special mission and his charismatic qualities. "I swear to you," he once told his grandson, Moses Ḥayyim Ephraim of Sodylkow, "that there is one

18

"Ḥasidim Dancing" by Chanoch Lieberman (1952). The Ba'al Shem Tov taught that prayer is acceptable only when it flows from a joyous heart, and Ḥasidim frequently express their joy through song and dance.

man in the world who hears Torah from God and the *Shekhinah*, and not from an angel or a seraph." Yet he feared failure, as is clear from the continuation of the above statement: "But he is not convinced that he will not be pushed aside by God, for he can easily be plummetted into the abyss of evil."

The Doctrine of Devekut

At the core of the Ba'al Shem Tov's teaching is the principle of *devekut* ("adhesion," "cleaving") although for him the term had far greater emotional content than in its earlier Kabbalistic usage. Declaring that "faith is the adhesion of the soul to God," he demanded that *devekut* be present in all daily acts. Man must worship God and cleave to Him not only when practicing religious acts and holy deeds, but also in his daily affairs, in his business, and in social contacts, for when a "man is occupied with material needs, yet his thought cleaves to God, he will be blessed."

Opposed Asceticism

Since the possibilities of achieving *devekut* were so widespread, there was no need to withdraw from worldly life or to stand aloof from society. Indeed, the Ba'al Shem Tov not only emphasized the element of joy in the worship of God, but he vigorously opposed fasts and asceticism, and he even advised rabbis and preachers not to resort to harsh admonition. He warned Jacob Joseph of Polonnoye "lest he bring himself to the danger of many fasts, which contribute to melancholy and sadness." According to the Ba'al Shem Tov, physical pleasure can give rise to spiritual pleasure, i.e., *devekut*. A physical act can be considered a religious act if the person performing it intends to worship God and the act is performed in a state of *devekut*. For the Ba'al Shem Tov as well as his disciples, *devekut* – especially during prayer – would often assume a decidedly ecstatic character.

Through prayer, the Ba'al Shem Tov taught, man can attain *devekut*, and make contact with the divine worlds. The way to *devekut* in prayer (as in the study of Torah) is through concentration on the mystical meaning of the letters. However, prayer that directs man to the attainment of *devekut* is at times disturbed by "alien thoughts" (*maḥashavot zarot*), and he who prays must deal with these properly, so that they do not frustrate his spiritual efforts. The Ba'al Shem Tov's particular way of dealing with "alien thoughts" came to be called "the wisdom of the Besht" and led Rabbi Naḥman of Horodenka to recognize his authority and join his group.

Alien Thoughts

Alien thoughts were derived from a heavenly source and were understood by the Ba'al Shem Tov to be the result of cosmic processes generally associated with the doctrine of the fallen holy sparks (*nizozot*) in Lurianic Kabbalah. These sparks of divine light are hidden in the extraneous ("sinful") thoughts and aspire to rise and be redeemed. This thrust conveys the undesirable thought to the human heart. He who sublimates the extraneous thought helps the spark return to its divine source (see page 36). Some alien thoughts must be sublimated and corrected; others must be repelled and removed. "If a man wishes to know how to distinguish between a thought to be repelled and one to be sublimated, he should contemplate whether correction to the thought entered his mind together with the extraneous thought, in which case he should seek to bring it close to him and sublimate it; but if he cannot immediately correct this thought then he must remove it."

Holy Sparks

From the areas of Podolia and Volhynia where he was active, the Ba'al Shem Tov's reputation spread even to circles unconnected with his religious leadership. That his activity also aroused opposition is evident from the legends about him and is hinted at in some of his parables. Rabbi Ḥayyim ha-Kohen Rappaport of Lvov warned his relatives in Buchach not to turn to "the witch doctor who calls himself Ba'al Shem."

A Witch Doctor?

The Ba'al Shem Tov did not put his teachings in writing and he even opposed the attempts of others to do so. But twenty

Ḥasidic women dancing, a charcoal sketch by Tully Filmus.

years after his death in 1760, his disciple Jacob Joseph of Polonnoye, presented in three of his own works hundreds of sermons and homilies that he had heard from the Ba'al Shem Tov. Other disciples, and their disciples, included in their works statements that they had heard from him or which had been cited in his name.

Fact and Legend

It is extremely difficult to disentangle fact from legend in studying the life and work of the Ba'al Shem Tov, but the message of the movement he founded is clear: simple faith is superior to scholasticism untouched with fervor, joy is to be invoked in God's service, and there are "holy sparks" in all things to be redeemed by a life of sanctity. The Besht, says Abraham Joshua Heschel, "brought Heaven down to earth. He and his disciples, the Ḥasidim, banished melancholy from the soul and uncovered the ineffable delight of being a Jew."

3. ḤASIDISM BECOMES A MOVEMENT

Although Rabbi Jacob Joseph of Polonnoye – the first theoretician of Ḥasidism – was the more senior disciple of the Ba'al Shem Tov, the latter passed the mantle of leadership on to Dov Baer, the "Maggid" ("Preacher") of Mezhirech (died 1772).

The Maggid of Mezhirech

An erudite talmudic scholar, Dov Baer also made a profound study of the Kabbalah, and at first he adopted an ascetic way of life. The mortifications to which he subjected himself before he embraced Ḥasidism eventually made him ill; he contracted a disease which affected his legs and confined him to his bed. Tradition relates that he sought a cure from the Ba'al Shem Tov, whose reputation as a healer was widespread, after which he became one of his foremost disciples. Dov Baer's conversion to Ḥasidism was an event of the utmost importance for the new

Joy among Ḥasidim, captured by Tully Filmus.

sect. Whereas during the life of the Ba'al Shem Tov the chief adherents of Ḥasidism were drawn from the lower classes of society, the Maggid succeeded in attracting some of the most learned scholars of the day. And they, in turn, directed their efforts mainly to winning over the educated circles of the Jews, though the uneducated were by no means excluded. Unlike the Ba'al Shem Tov, Dov Baer was not a man of the people, and his illness made it difficult for him to associate with his disciples. He too possessed charismatic qualities, however, and was an eloquent preacher and teacher. He was highly esteemed by his disciples, who not only derived spiritual sustenance from his teachings and utterances but also divined an inner significance in his daily life.

Attracts the Scholars

"I did not go to the Maggid of Mezhirech to learn interpretations of the Torah from him," said Aryeh Leib Sarahs (1730-91), "but to note his way of tying his shoelaces and taking off his shoes. For of what worth are the meanings given to the Torah, after all? In his actions, in his speech, in his bearing, and in his fealty to the Lord, man must make the Torah manifest."

Dov Baer transferred the center of Ḥasidism from Podolia in southeast Poland to Volhynia in the center, and this facilitated its spread throughout the country. From the Maggid's court, missionaries went forth who were successful in attracting many scholars to Ḥasidism and sending them to the master at Mezhirech to absorb his teaching. From the new center in Volhynia, Ḥasidism thus spread northward into Belorussia and

Studying Talmud. The Ba'al Shem Tov had stressed ecstasy; when Dov Baer, the Maggid of Mezhirech, turned to Ḥasidism, the emphasis on study and learning was restored.

Two distinct facial expressions have been captured in these oil paintings by Isidor Kaufmann (1853-1921). The pensive face above is that of "An East European Jewess," while a somber awe rests on the features of the "Old Jew with Torah." The loose white gown or *kitel* that he wears under his *tallit* indicates that it is probably the Day of Atonement.

The legal arguments of the Talmud are commonly debated by pairs of scholars or in small groups. "Study," an oil painting by Leopold Pilichowski (1869-1933), shows a Ḥasidic sage endeavoring to convince a colleague of his interpretation of one of the points of the Law.

Lithuania and westward into Galicia, and it took root in central Poland; more, it succeeded in penetrating the center of the opposition, Vilna. Many local Ḥasidic leaders became influential as communal leaders and local rabbis. Dov Baer's activity may be considered the beginning of Ḥasidism as a movement while his personal conduct set the precedent in Ḥasidism for the institution of the ẓaddik, or saintly leader. He enjoyed respect and authority outside his own community, and his reputation as a Talmudist led many Jews to turn to him with questions of civil law.

Even in Vilna

A disciple gave this account of the Great Maggid : "When we journeyed to him, most of our desires were stilled upon entering town. Whoever had a particularly keen desire was soothed upon entering the Maggid's house. But if there was one among us whose soul was still rocking like a boat, when he beheld the Maggid's face he came to rest."

No Absolute Evil

Though by and large Dov Baer adopted the Lurianic Kabbalah, he did not accept the Lurianic dualism which accentuates the extremes of evil and good; for him there is no absolute evil but only degrees of good. "Sin contains repentance," he said, "as the olive contains the oil. At the hour of thy repentance and of thy turning away from sin, the sparks of divine splendor that were in it are raised to the heavenly regions."

Pride and Humility

Humility is counted by the Ḥasidim as one of the chief virtues, and Dov Baer took pains to inculcate it in his disciples. One Ḥasidic tale relates that before the Maggid began to teach the two brothers, Shmelke and Pinḥas, he told them how to conduct themselves throughout the day, from the moment of waking to falling asleep. His directions took into account all their habits, confirming them or modifying them, as though he knew the whole of their lives. In closing he said: "And before you lie down at night, you add up everything you have done during the day. And when a man calculates his hours and sees that he has not wasted a moment in idleness, when his heart beats high with

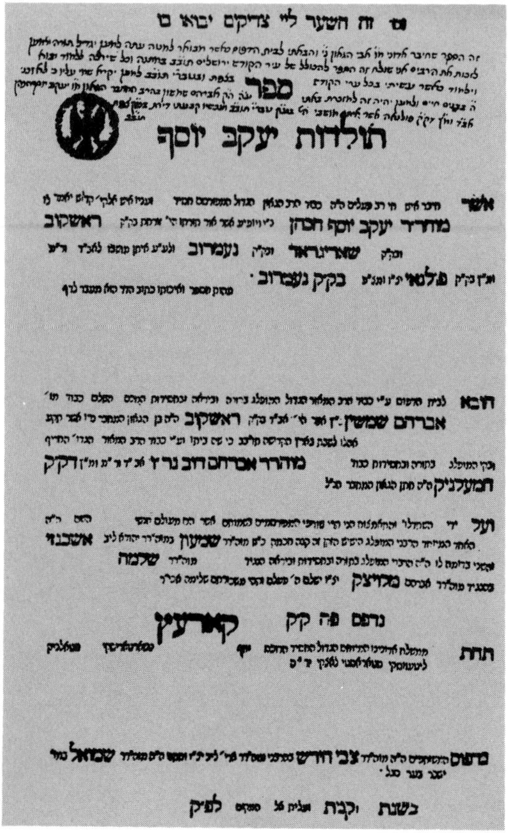
זה השער לה' צדיקים יבואו בו

ספר

תולדות יעקב יוסף

אשר ... מוהר"ר יעקב יוסף הכהן ... ראשקוב

שארגראד ... נעמרוב

פלנאי ... בקק נעמרוב

הבא ... אברהם שמשון ... ראשקוב

מוהר"ר אברהם דוב בער ... דקק

המעלניק

ועל ... שמעון ... אשכנזי

שלמה

מדריצק

נדפס פה קק קארעץ

תחת

מדפיס ... צבי הירש ... שמואל

בשנת וקבת ... לפ"ק

Title page of *Toledot Ya'akov Yosef,* by Jacob Joseph, Ḥasidism's first theoretician. It contains the basic teachings of Ḥasidism, including some the author heard from the Ba'al Shem Tov.

pride, then – up in Heaven – they take all his good works, crush them into a ball, and hurl it down into the abyss."

In the Maggid's later years, Ḥasidism aroused fierce opposition on the part of many rabbis. Especial targets of their hostility were the new movement's ecstatic mode of religious worship, the changes introduced in the prayer ritual and the neglect of Torah study by the youth who abandoned the yeshivot and flocked to Mezhirech. Eventually a ban of excommunication was pronounced on Ḥasidism in Vilna the stronghold of the Mitnaggedim.

Tradition has it that the excommunication affected Dov Baer's health and he died shortly afterward.

Jacob Joseph of Polonnoye

Dov Baer's missionary activity on behalf of Ḥasidism was complemented by the literary activity of his contemporary, Rabbi Jacob Joseph of Polonnoye (died c. 1782). When Jacob Joseph came under the influence of the Ba'al Shem Tov in 1741 he was rabbi of Shargorod, the second largest community of Podolia. His Ḥasidic leanings embroiled him in a controversy with his community, as a result of which he was expelled from Shargorod around 1748. His failure to succeed the Ba'al Shem Tov in the leadership of the Ḥasidic movement is said to have embittered him.

Polish children at the beginning of the 19th century. After J.P. Norblin *Collections de Costumes Polonaises,* 1817.

Group of Ḥasidic boys in Cracow, Poland. The casquettes they are wearing was the standard form of headcovering for Ḥasidic children.

The 'Toledot' Raises a Storm

We have already referred to Jacob Joseph's first and principal work, *Toledot Ya'akov Yosef*. This contains homilies of the author as well as "words that I heard from my teacher," i.e., the Ba'al Shem Tov. It is the first work to express the basic teachings of Ḥasidism, both in a positive formulation as well as in the bitter criticism it contains of the traditional Jewish leadership and its scale of values. The publication of *Toledot Ya'akov Yosef* aroused the wrath of the Mitnaggedim, and copies of it were apparently burned in Brody. The homilies of Jacob Joseph reveal him as leader of a community, as well as a penetrating and incisive theoretician and social critic.

The presence of God is manifest everywhere and in each and every human thought, Jacob Joseph taught. Even "when man is engaged in prayer and an alien and evil thought enters his mind, it has come to man so that he may improve and uplift it. If he does not believe in this then his acceptance of the rule of the Kingdom of Heaven is defective because, Heaven forfend, he thereby restricts His presence." The ultimate purpose of man is "Thou shalt cleave to Him." This adhesion is only possible through joy; fasting and self-affliction bring sorrow, and sorrow is the root of all evil. Prayers should be recited with a purified and concentrated mind and with joy.

Sorrow the Root of All Evil

This, however, was only after Jacob Joseph came under the influence of the Ba'al Shem Tov. Before that, like Dov Baer, he had practiced asceticism, fasting every day until nightfall and for one week a month, until midnight. But the Ba'al Shem Tov ordered him to stop, "for this way is dark and bitter and leads to depression and melancholy. The glory of God does not dwell where there is depression but where the joy in performing His *mitzvah* prevails."

Decentralization of Leadership

After the death of the great Maggid, Ḥasidism remained without a single leader commanding the same authority and general support from all Ḥasidim, and the leadership was assumed by a number of his disciples. It was in this third generation of the movement (c. 1773-1815) that the basic pattern of Ḥasidic leadership and succession emerged. There were a number of factors that contributed to the decentralization of leadership in the Ḥasidic world and consequently to an evergrowing diversification in Ḥasidic thought and in the Ḥasidic way of life: the spread and growth of Ḥasidism, the diversified and illustrious leadership of charismatic individuals who became heads of local centers, each developing his own style of teaching and interpreting the Ḥasidic way of life, the breakup of former lines of communication and of

Diversity of Style

cultural ties caused by the partitions of Poland-Lithuania (1772, 1793 and 1795), and finally the pressures brought to bear on Ḥasidic communities by the struggle against the movement. From this generation onward there were always a number of contemporaneous leaders, each claiming the allegiance of his followers. For the most part, both leadership and allegiance were handed down from generation to generation and thus there arose both the dynasties of Ḥasidic ẓaddikim and the hereditary camps of their followers. At times the living charismatic force asserted itself anew, as in the case of Jacob Isaac, the "Seer" of Lublin, who began to lead a community during the lifetime of his master, Elimelech of Lyzhansk, without his blessing, and of Jacob Isaac of Przysucha, the Seer's disciple, who led a community in the lifetime of his master, though without leaving him.

Tension and Rivalry

In this third generation, the new pattern of leadership assured the victory of Ḥasidism over its opponents and its increasing spread throughout Eastern Europe. With the inclusion of Galicia in the Austrian Empire, Ḥasidism also gained adherents among Hungarian Jewry. At this time Ḥasidism also developed systematic schools of theology, such as the more intellectual and study-centered Ḥabad Ḥasidism. Some Ḥasidic personalities, like Levi Isaac of Berdichev, were venerated by all Jewry as models of piety and love of humanity. The spiritual outlook and pattern of leadership of the practical ẓaddik also crystallized in this generation. With such diversification in leadership and attitudes, it is not to be wondered that from this generation on there was considerable and undisguised tension between the various Ḥasidic courts and dynasties, which sometimes flared up into bitter and prolonged conflicts.

Wins Legitimacy

By the 1830s the main surge of the spread of Ḥasidism was spent. From a persecuted sect it had become the way of life and the leadership structure of the majority of Jews in the Ukraine, Galicia, and central Poland, and it had sizable groups of followers in Belorussia-Lithuania and Hungary. With the great waves of emigration to the West beginning in 1881, Ḥasidism was carried to Western Europe and to an even greater extent to the United States. In the West its character was gradually, but ever more rapidly, diluted and its influence became more external and formal. With the abatement of the struggle against Ḥasidism by the end of its third generation and its acceptance as part of the Orthodox camp, Ḥasidism attained the distinction of being the first religious trend in Judaism since the days of the Second Temple which had a self-defined way of life and a distinctive rite of worship but yet was acknowledged (albeit somewhat grudgingly) by those who differed from it as a legitimate Jewish phenomenon.

4. CLEAVING TO GOD

Many of Ḥasidism's basic ideas are rooted in earlier Jewish sources – Kabbalistic literature in particular – but it nevertheless produced much that was new if only by emphasis. With few exceptions, Ḥasidic ideas are not presented systematically in the Ḥasidic writings, but an examination of these writings reveals certain patterns common to all the Ḥasidic masters.

'Thou Shalt Cleave to Him'

It is generally agreed that the central tendency of Ḥasidic teaching is *devekut*, meaning "adhesion" or "cleaving" to God. "There is one *mitzvah* in the Torah which includes everything," said Jacob Joseph of Polonnoye, "and that is 'Thou shalt cleave unto Him.' " In Kabbalistic literature the usual meaning of *devekut* is "communion with God," which is achieved mainly during the time of prayer or meditation before prayer through using the right *kavvanot*, the mystical interpretations and meanings given to the words of prayer. There *devekut* is usually described as the highest step on a spiritual ladder, which is reached after the believer has mastered the attitudes of fear of God, love of God, and so forth. In Ḥasidism, however, *devekut* became not only the

As the soul of the worshiper leaps in ecstasy to its Divine Source, so some of the Ḥasidic sects encouraged violent movements in prayer. This painting of a Ḥasid dancing is by Agadati (1923).

supreme achievement of religious life but also its starting point. *Devekut*, according to the Ḥasidim, should be the believer's constant state of mind, not only during the high points of prayer and religious activity but even when he is engaged in the everyday affairs of life.

Consecration of the Everyday

Beginning with the Ba'al Shem Tov, we find the Ḥasidic masters advocating the hallowing of all life. In whatever he is doing, man must dedicate himself to God. "The outer world no longer stood as an obstacle to the service of God, it became a means for the service of the Creator." This ideal of the consecration of the everyday is the point of many Ḥasidic tales.

Thus, Rabbi Naḥman of Kossov, a disciple of the Ba'al Shem Tov, taught that we should always have the Lord in our thoughts.

Two young boys studying together in *ḥeder* in Poland, before the Second World War.

He was asked whether this was possible when a man was engaged in buying and selling. "Of course we can," Naḥman answered. "If we are able to think of business when we are praying, we should be able to think of praying when we are doing business."

As Good as Prayer

When a teamster asked Rabbi Levi Isaac of Berdichev whether he should give up his occupation because it interfered with regular attendance at the synagogue, the Rabbi asked him whether he carried poor travelers free of charge. The teamster said that he did. "Then," ruled the Rabbi, "you serve the Lord in your occupation just as faithfully as you would by frequenting the synagogue."

Rabbi Menaḥem Mendel of Kotzk once astonished a number of learned visitors when he posed the question: "Where is the dwelling of God?" They laughed: "What a thing to ask! Is not the whole world filled with His glory?" Then he gave his own answer to his question: "God dwells wherever man lets Him in."

Ḥasidism, in other words, denied the existence of a dichotemy between the life of the spirit and life in the world. The Ba'al Shem Tov interpreted the verse "In all thy ways know Him" thus: "Even in every bodily thing that you do it is necessary that it be a service of a higher need . . . all for the sake of heaven." In Ḥasidic parlance this doctrine is known as *avodah be-gashmiyyut* ("the service of God through corporeality"): the human physical dimension is regarded as an area in which man is capable of religious behavior. Man should not be overly concerned with the upper world, but "in this lower world, the world of corporeality, let the hidden life of God shine forth."

In This Lower World

Ḥanokh of Aleksandrow (1798-1870) gave a unique interpretation to the verse in the Psalms: "The heavens are the hea-

vens of the Lord, but the earth hath He given to the children of men." It goes thus: "The heavens are the heavens of the Lord – you see they are already of a heavenly character. 'But the earth hath He given to the children of men' – so that they might make of it something heavenly."

Consecration of All Things

The Ḥasidic concept of corporeal worship has been poetically explained by Martin Buber: "One eats in consecration, one savors one's food in consecration, and the table becomes an altar. One works in consecration and lifts the sparks that are hidden in all tools [vessels]. One walks over the fields in consecration, and the silent songs of all creatures, those they speak to God, enter into the song of one's own soul. One drinks to one's companions in consecration, each to the other, and it is as if one studies together with them in the Torah. One dances in consecration, and a splendor radiates over the community. A man is united with his wife in consecration, and the *Shekhinah* rests over them."

In the teachings of the Ba'al Shem Tov the doctrine of worship through corporeality was carried to the extreme, culminating in the tenet that man must worship God with both the good and evil in his nature. It was man's duty to 'transform' evil into good, through an actual confrontation of evil in its own domain.

Don't Alarm the Thief

If you discover at night that a thief has crept into your house, and cry out, the thief will flee, and it is all as if nothing had happened. It is better not to alarm the thief but let him draw near until you can lay hold of him and bind him. For then, instead of merely driving away the evil, you transform it into good.

The Limits of Worship through Corporeality

Dov Baer, the Maggid of Mezhirech, conceived of *avodah be-gashmiyyut* as indispensable, although he covertly questioned whether every man was permitted to engage in it. In fact, a pupil of one of the Maggid's disciples, Meshullam Feivush of Zbarazh, specifically states that it was not the Maggid's intention to proclaim *avodah be-gashmiyyut* as a general practice but rather as one intended for spiritually superior individuals who would be

The community is a living organism with the ẓaddik as its soul; the Munkaceve rebbe and his disciples in Poland before the Second World War.

immune to the danger of the concept's vulgarization. One of the Maggid's most important disciples, Shneur Zalman of Lyady, mentions the practice with a touch of derision. Nevertheless, it came to occupy a central place in Ḥasidic literature. The meaning and limits of the concept served as a focal point of an ongoing controversy among the movement's adherents.

Prayer – A Mystical Encounter with God

Prayer in Ḥasidism is a mystical encounter with the Divine, the heart leaping in ecstasy to its Source. Violent movements in prayer were not unusual; some of the Ḥasidic groups even encouraged their followers to turn somersaults during their prayers. Prayer is frequently seen in Ḥasidism as man's most important religious activity. Rabbi Shneur Zalman of Lyady, the founder of the intellectual Ḥabad sect in Ḥasidism, wrote: "For although the forms of the prayers and the duty of praying three times a day are rabbinic, the idea of prayer is the foundation of the whole Torah."

A man at prayer in the view of Ḥasidism, finds himself in conflict with the external world. Said Ze'ev Wolf of Zhitomer (died 1800): "All the thoughts and associations with which he busied himself when he went out to his work and his business . . . and talked and bargained with the uncircumcised: now at the time of study and prayer they rise before his eyes, and these are the very 'alien thoughts' that come to man at the time of study and prayer." Prayer requires a great effort of concentration if man is to overcome the tendency of external reality to permeate his consciousness. This quite natural tendency is considered in Ḥasidism as the "wayfaring" of thought and as such is the very opposite of its concentration, which requires a turning away from the world and which is based on man's ability to achieve pure introspection devoid of all content. The function of this introspection is to achieve the utter voiding ("annihilation") of human thought and to uplift the element of divinity latent in

Annihilate Human Thought

Early Ḥasidim held that *devekut* while studying, in the sense of intense concentration on the letters of the text, could reveal on earth the divine forces by which God governs the world. Painting by Lazar Krestin (1902).

man's soul. The transformation of this element from a latent to an active condition is understood as true union with God, the state marking the climax of *devekut*. "Do you wish to know what is proper prayer?" asked Jacob Isaac of Przysucha. "When you are so engrossed that you do not feel a knife thrust into your body, then you are offering prayer aright." The spiritual effort involved in prayer was considered so strenuous as to give rise to the Ḥasidic dictum, "I give thanks to God that I remain alive after praying." It was said of Uri ben Pinḥas of Strelisk (died 1826) that every day before saying his prayers he bade farewell to his wife and family for fear that he might die of ecstasy in the middle of his devotions.

For Ḥasidism prayer is primarily a ladder by means of which man can ascend to *devekut* and union with the Divinity. The individualistic tendencies inherent in prayer through *devekut*, however, did not lead the Ḥasidim to belittle the importance of communal worship, nor did they demand of the Ḥasid that he achieve *devekut* outside the bounds of the community and the halakhic framework of prayer. But many Ḥasidic groups, otherwise strictly conformist, disregarded the laws governing prayer at fixed times on the grounds that these interfere with the need for adequate preparation and with the spontaneity which is part of the prayer's essence. "In Kotsk," said Rabbi Menaḥem Mendel, "we have a soul and not a clock." It was not long, however, before the Ḥasidim felt themselves in danger of jeopardizing the framework of the *halakhah* and, for the most part, they recanted and accepted the authority of the existing frameworks.

A Soul and Not a Clock

Devekut, which became the banner under which Ḥasidism went forth to revitalize religious life and modify the time-honored hierarchy of values in Judaism, quickly led to a confrontation between it and the daily pattern of existence of the Ḥasid. It was not only traditional worship that was brought face to face with new problems; the same held true for Torah study. There was not a fundamental revolt against the study of Torah as such, and few Ḥasidic masters subscribed to the view of Menaḥem Mendel of Peremyshlany (born 1728), an early follower of the Ba'al Shem Tov, that Torah study and the practice

A New Scale of Values

of devotion were incompatible. ("If we divert our thoughts from devotion to God," he said, "and study excessively, we will forget the fear of Heaven.") But Ḥasidism did challenge the traditional notion that Torah study – *talmud torah* – is the supreme religious duty of the Jew. And *devekut* laid claim to so large a part of man's day that little time was left for learning. Pinḥas of Karitz, of the circle of the Ba'al Shem Tov, gave a picturesque definition of the new hierarchy of values: "I am in constant fear that I shall turn out to be wiser than I am pious."

Torah li-Shemah

For the Ba'al Shem Tov, the study of Torah was not an end in itself. The Torah should be studied, not for the sake of acquiring knowledge, but in order to learn the true service of God from it. The early Ḥasidic masters accused the conventional scholars of engaging in Torah study for motives of fame, wealth and prestige – and hence, of not living up to the rabbinic ideal of *Torah li-shemah*, i.e., the Torah should not be studied from any worldly motives but "for its own sake." But early Ḥasidism went much further and gave the very concept of *Torah li-shemah* an entirely new interpretation. It now was said to mean *devekut* while studying, especially in the sense that intense concentration on the letters of the text could reveal on earth the divine forces by means of which God governs the world. The comparatively large number of classical talmudic scholars among the second and third generations of Ḥasidic masters, however, prevented any radical departure from the older ideal.

Even the importance of the *mitzvot* was overshadowed by *devekut* since the fulfillment of the *mitzvot* was assessed in terms of the *devekut* achieved by man. "Performance of the *mitzvah* without *devekut* is meaningless" was a widespread Ḥasidic slogan. In the new scale of values the *mitzvah* itself became a means – and only one of several – to *devekut*. "The reason why we should do what the Law commands is not to gain grace thereby in the eyes of God, but to learn how to love God and to be united to Him. The important thing is not how many separate injunctions are obeyed, but how and in what spirit we obey them. The object of fulfilling these various ordinances is to put oneself, as it were, on the same plane with God, and thus, in the ordinary phrase of the religious mystic, to become one with Him."

A Gospel of Joy and Optimism

Ḥasidism preached a gospel of joy, optimism and self-worth through religious experience. Aaron of Karlin (1736-72), the

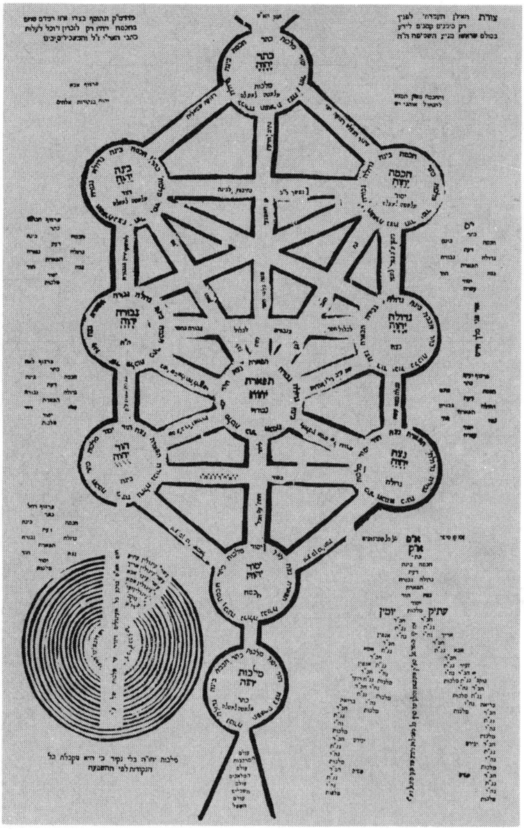

The ten *sefirot* (emanations) from God according to kabbalistic theory represented in the form of a tree. The diagram at the lower left is probably a cross-section of a tree trunk.

"A Jew," by Isidor Kaufmann.

"Portrait of a Young Man," by Isidor Kaufmann.

A Ḥasidic family in Jerusalem sets out for a stroll on Purim morning to deliver the *mishlo'aḥ manot,* the traditional food gifts which are exchanged by friends

pioneer of Ḥasidism in Lithuania, regarded melancholy as "the lowest abyss." He taught that the Jew who does not rejoice in being a Jew is ungrateful to Heaven. The Maggid of Mezhirech employed the following homily: "When a king is at a celebration he can be approached by many people who otherwise would be denied entrance to the palace. Likewise when we serve God with joy, he is more approachable." Ḥanokh of Aleksandrow underscored the importance of joy with these words: "Do you wish to know how important it is to be full of joy at all times? Moses enumerated a long series of curses (Deuteronomy 28) and explained in verse 47: ". . .because you did not serve the Lord your God with joyfulness, and with gladness of heart."

Ḥasidic optimism and joy are based on the notion that there is nothing in the universe but God. Rabbi Menaḥem Mendel, the third rabbi of Lubavich, observed that the disciples of the Ba'al Shem Tov gave the "very profound" turn to the doctrine of the oneness of God so that it means not only that He is unique, as the medieval thinkers said, but that He is all that is; there is no reality in created things. For if the world and its sorrows do not enjoy true existence and the divine light and vitality pervade all, what cause is there for despair or despondency? When man rejoices that he has been called to serve God, he bestirs the divine joy in heaven and blessing flows through all creation. A melancholy frame of mind is anathema to Ḥasidism, serving only to create a barrier between man and his Maker. Rabbi Naḥman of Bratslav held that dejection is one of the major reasons for man's drifting away from God, which in turn leads him to sin.

Nothing but God

Even over his sins a man should not grieve overmuch: "At times the evil inclination misleads man into thinking that he has committed a serious sin when it was actually nothing but a peccadillo or no sin at all, the intention having been to bring man into a state of melancholy," the Ba'al Shem Tov taught. "But melancholy is a great hindrance to God's service. Even if a man has stumbled and sinned he should not become too sad because

Danger of Melancholy

this will prevent him from worshiping God." Aaron the Second, of Karlin, (died 1872) taught that "repentance comes essentially out of joy and delight."

Like a Bird Without Wings

The study of the Torah, prayer, and other religious duties must be carried out in love and fear, Ḥasidism teaches. The bare deed without the love and fear of God is like a bird without wings. A Ḥasidic tale relates that the Ba'al Shem Tov could not bring himself to enter a certain synagogue because it was full of lifeless prayers which, lacking the wings of love and fear, were unable to ascend to heaven. As observant Jews the Ḥasidim did not seek to deny the value of the deed as such but they repeatedly taught that the deed could be elevated only when carried out in a spirit of devotion. Ḥayyim of Czernowitz writes: "There is a man whose love for his God is so strong and faithful that he carries out each *mitzvah* with superlative excellence, strength and marvelous power, waiting in longing to perform the *mitzvah*, his soul expiring in yearning. . . . Such a man's *mitzvot* are those which fly ever upward in joy and satisfaction to draw down from there every kind of blessing and flow of grace to all worlds."

Redeem the Sparks

This idea was applied to all of man's deeds, and not to his religious obligations alone. In all things there are "holy sparks" (*niẓoẓot*) waiting to be redeemed and rescued for sanctity by man's using his appetites to serve God. The most profane action can be done in holiness, and when a man performs it in holiness he praises the sparks. Even the taste of food is a reflection (albeit a pale one) of the spiritual force that brings the food into being. Man should be led on by it to contemplate the divine vitality in the food and thus to God Himself. In the words of the highly charged mythology of the Lurianic Kabbalah, the "holy sparks" released by man provide the *Shekhinah* (the Divine Presence which resides in this world) with her "female waters" which, in turn, cause the flow of the "male waters" and thus help "the unification of the Holy One, blessed be He, and His *Shekhinah*" to produce cosmic harmony. Because of the significance of man's role in the sacred marriage and its importance in the Ḥasidic scheme, the Ḥasidim adopted from the Kabbalists the formula: "For the sake of the unification of the Holy One, blessed be He, and His *Shekhinah*" (*le-shem yiḥud . . .*) before the performance of every *mitzvah*. (The redemption of the "holy sparks" was one of the reasons given for Ḥasidic fondness for tobacco. Smoking a pipe served to release subtle "sparks" not otherwise accessible.) According to Gershom Scholem, the doctrine of the holy sparks is "probably the most important legacy of the Lurianic Kabbalah to Ḥasidism."

5. THE ẒADDIK

Is the program of sustained contemplation and utter devotion to God that has been sketched in the last few pages really possible for all men? For the most part the Ḥasidic answer is in the negative. That is why the doctrine of ẓaddikism is so important for Ḥasidism. The holy man – the ẓaddik – his thoughts constantly on God, uplifts the prayers of his followers and all their other thoughts and actions.

The ẓaddik must simultaneously observe the *mitzvah* of *devekut* and maintain contact with the world about him. Rabbi Ḥayyim Mordecai Rosenbaum (b.1904).

The doctrine of the ẓaddik was first set forth in Jacob Joseph of Polonnoye's *Toledot Ya'akov Yosef* which, as we have already noted, consists to a large extent of the teachings of the Ba'al Shem Tov, and which is regarded as the most important work in the entire Ḥasidic literature. Later Ḥasidic masters made alterations in this doctrine and, in practice, the character of the ẓaddik and his relations with his followers differed from one Ḥasidic court to another.

The Intermediary Between God and Israel

Jacob Joseph describes the ẓaddik, like Moses, as the intermediary between God and Israel. He is the "channel" through which the constant spiritual outpouring (*shefa*) from heaven is

General view of the eastern wall of the Bratslav synagogue in Jerusalem.

The chair of Reb Naḥman of Bratslav. No rabbi succeeded Reb Naḥman as rebbe of the Bratslaver Ḥasidim, and they continue to venerate only him. (For this reason they are sometimes called the Toite [Dead] Ḥasidim.) Reb Naḥman's chair is used only at circumcision ceremonies when the infant is laid on it briefly. When the Bratslaver Ḥasidim fled Europe at the outbreak of the Nazi terror, the chair was broken up and each piece was separately smuggled to Israel by the Bratslavers. In Israel in 1936 they grouped together once again and reassembled the chair. It now stands in the Bratslav synagogue in the Mea Shearim quarter of Jerusalem.

transmitted to the people. And this function of transmission is an indispensable aspect of the ẓaddik's task. "If he who receives *shefa* does not hand it over to others, it will be cut off from him as well. . . . If he wants to receive he must give to others." In the opposite direction, too, the ẓaddik is the intermediary; he enables the people to attain *devekut*, to draw close to God. For not every man is capable of achieving *devekut* by his own efforts. Most individuals will find it necessary to cleave to the ẓaddik, and then be raised with him to the stage of cleaving to God.

Gives and Receives

But just as the people need the ẓaddik, the ẓaddik needs the people; alone each is incomplete. Each of them is only a half, and they require one another as a man and his wife. The ẓaddik is likened to the head or the eyes of the body, and the multitude to the feet. The community is thus conceived as a living organism, the ẓaddik being its life and soul in his generation. And the interrelationship in this corporate body is such that any failure on the part even of the lowest member will be reflected – and to a far more damaging degree – in the state of "the head" – the ẓaddik. None of the members can cleave truly to God so long as even one of them is not conscious of his need to be uplifted through the head. Hence it is the duty of the ẓaddik to exert his influence over each and every one in his community.

A Living Organism

A Mystic in the Community of Men

In order to fulfill his destiny the ẓaddik must achieve what Scholem has called the paradox of being a mystic in the community of men. For he must simultaneously observe the *mitzvah* of *devekut* and maintain contact with the material world through the circle about him, even those who are counted as sinners. Not for him is the sanctuary of the House of Study or the solitude of a monastic cell. Spiritually alone with God, he is the center of his community. He influences society and is influenced by it. The sins of his contemporaries affect him and reduce his stature, while his sinful thoughts stimulate others to sin. The task of the

A *farbrengen* (gathering) of Ḥabad Ḥasidim in Brooklyn, New York. The present rebbe, Menaḥem Mendel Schneersohn, is seated at the center of the table and is leaning forward to speak to some of his Ḥasidim. A *farbrengen* is a gathering of Ḥasidim in the presence of the rebbe in celebration of occasions and anniversaries important to the group.

ẓaddik is to teach the people to worship God by means of *devekut* and to bring sinners to repentance.

Descent of the Ẓaddik

Moreover, for the sake of this unification with the multitude, and in order to be able to uplift it, a ẓaddik may sometimes have to descend from his own level and sin. This concept of the "descent of the ẓaddik" – which has its origin in Kabbalistic literature – holds an important place in the teachings of Jacob Joseph of Polonnoye. He illustrates it by the famous parable of the king's son.

Left : Rabbi Jacob Joseph Twersky, surrounded by his followers. Rabbi Twersky died in 1968.
Right : The Klausenburger rebbe reciting *havdalah* at the conclusion of the Sabbath.

The King's Son

A king sent his only son away from the royal palace to a village so that he might afterward yearn all the more for his father's table. Because of his foolishness, the prince mingled with the strangers in the village, learned their ways and, after a time, forgot the royal pleasures. The king sent one of his nobles after the prince to bring him back, but he failed. Another was sent, and then another and another, but none succeeded. At last one of the nobles discovered the secret. He removed his elegant clothing and put on plain clothes like those of the villagers, in order that he might have something in common with the prince and enter into conversation with him. He succeeded, and returned him to his father.

The ẓaddik, in other words, must stoop to conquer. He descends spiritually to the sinner, associates with him, and by his own ascent raises him and restores him to goodness, aiding him in purifying himself of his blemishes. "He is like one," said Levi Isaac of Berdichev, "who would raise his fellow from slime and rubbish: he too must go down near the slime and rubbish to raise him up." For if the ẓaddik himself is free of sin and guilt, he will be unable to raise up the multitude. He is like a broom: in order to sweep clean it must come in contact with dirt. "Thus Caleb joined himself to the spies, saying that he agreed with them, so that in the end, he was able to silence them."

Down to the Slime

It is said in the Ethics of the Fathers: "The boldfaced go to hell, the shamefaced to paradise." Rabbi Zusya expounded these words as follows: "The bold is he whom men call the ẓaddik; his sanctity emboldens him to descend hellward to carry aloft that which is low; he is not afraid of wickedness on the streets and at county fairs. But the shamefaced who fears infection must continually keep on a level with paradise; he must always pray and study and shun contact with those whom the ẓaddik lifts from the mire."

The Ẓaddik Descends to Hell

Jacob Joseph enjoins the ordinary Jew to believe in the ẓaddik with absolute faith, without any afterthoughts or doubts as to the ẓaddik's way of life, because all his actions are performed for the sake of heaven. The "man of matter" must also support the ẓaddik financially to enable him to fulfill his task successfully and devote himself to God through Torah study and prayer.

Practical Ẓaddikism

Elimelech of Lyzhansk (1717-87), a disciple of the Maggid of Mezhirech, offered another rationale for the support of the ẓaddik by his followers: this financial assistance was not for the ẓaddik's sake but for the sake of those privileged to help him. By supporting the ẓaddik with their worldly goods his Ḥasidim become attached to him through his dependence on them, which he readily accepts in his love for them. Their welfare thus becomes his, and his prayers on their behalf can be more readily answered. Elimelech is considered the theoretician and creator of "practical ẓaddikism." In his comprehensive work of ẓaddikism, *Noam Elimelekh* (1787), the ẓaddik appears as a spiritual superman, with the power to work miracles. He is the man to whom God has given control of the universe by his prayers. He even has power over life and death. God may have decreed that a person should die but this can be nullified by the prayers of the ẓaddik.

A Spiritual Superman

A disciple of Elimelech's, Jacob Isaac ("the Seer") of Lublin (1745-1815), likewise emphasized the practical work of the ẓaddik, his duty to care for the "life and livelihood" of his "children," the Ḥasidic congregation. Believing that material abundance preceded spiritual wealth, he held that to help a person repent it was first necessary to help him obtain his material needs. The ẓaddik ought "to extend great abundance and a comfortable living so that the people will be free to worship God." He is reported as having said that when the body enjoys plenty the soul too enjoys spiritual richness. But this accent on the ẓaddik's need to care for the multitude of Ḥasidim alienated those Lublin Ḥasidim who thought that the stress should be put on the aspiration toward spiritual perfection and constant *devekut*, who regarded the Ḥasidic ẓaddik as a guide to divine worship and not as a miracle worker. This atmosphere of "practical ẓaddikism" cultivated by the Seer was the background to his controversy with his most outstanding disciple, Jacob Isaac of Przysucha (1746-1814), known as *ha-Yehudi ha-Kadosh*, "the Holy Jew," who eventually left his master and gathered around him disciples of his own. The controversy divided Polish Ḥasidism for many years.

The Body Before the Soul

Jekuthiel Judah Halberstam of Klausenburg at the Western Wall with his followers.

A unique theory of the ẓaddik is that of Naḥman of Bratslav (1772-1811), a great-grandson of the Ba'al Shem Tov. It maintains that there is only one true ẓaddik – Naḥman himself – who is destined to be the Messiah. The Moses-like ẓaddik gives redemptive force to the prayers of the general community. The great ẓaddik's reflection on heretical questions may bring about the spiritual elevation of those who were formerly sunk in error. Even the *niggun* (Ḥasidic melody) sung by the ẓaddik has a similar influence. The biblical injunction, "I have set the Lord always before me" also applies to the Hasid's relationship with the zaddik. It is necessary to acknowledge that the "ẓaddik simulates his Creator," and that "through his teachings the ẓaddik teaches the Holy One, blessed be He, how to deal with us." The ẓaddik lives eternally, as it were, regardless of where he dwells, on earth or in the grave. A man must travel to the ẓaddik because "the main thing is what he hears from the mouth of the ẓaddik." Naḥman strongly emphasizes the obligation of confession before the ẓaddik and advocates praising him. Since the ẓaddik embodies all that is happening in the earthly and divine worlds, communication with him advances the processes of *tikkun* that Lurianic Kabbalah demands of Jews.

Naḥman of Bratslav

Is the Mediation of the Ẓaddik Indispensable?

On the other hand, there were leading Ḥasidic masters who held that the mediation of the ẓaddik was not indispensable. Thus, Dov Baer of Mezhirech held that every man can achieve direct contact with the Divine. While Dov Baer agreed with Jacob Joseph of Polonnoye that the ẓaddik is an intercessor for the bestowal of *shefa*, he regarded the social function of the ẓaddik as being on a lower plane than his mystical activity, in which he struggles to attain a life of utter holiness. There are even ẓaddikim who are compelled to withdraw from the people, Dov Baer maintained, because their contact with society is liable to result in their downfall. (When the Maggid realized that he had become known to the world, he begged God to tell him what sin of his had brought this punishment upon him.) Even Jacob Joseph of Polonnoye does not consistently describe the ẓaddik's mediation as a *sine qua non*. From some of his statements on the subject it would appear that only if one is unable to achieve *devekut* on his own should he seek to achieve it through the ẓaddik. In Ḥabad Ḥasidism the leadership of the ẓaddik is mainly spiritual: encounters between him and his Ḥasidim are devoted to the study of Torah and ethics and to discussion of the problems of the community.

Remedies and Amulets

In practice, however, most ẓaddikim (or rebbes) were regarded by their Ḥasidim as wonder-healers, oracles and miracle workers (see page 11). One of the most prominent of these was Israel of Kozienice (1733-1814), also known as the Maggid of Koznitz, who gained great popularity as a "practical ẓaddik," actively assisting his Ḥasidim with their family problems and in their struggle to make a livelihood; he even distributed remedies and amulets. For this activity he was sharply criticized by the Mitnaggedim, while the Ḥasidim justified it, explaining that the amulets contained his name only. According to one Ḥasidic tale, Israel's disciples informed him one day that an elderly woman had borne a son even though she had not gone to a rebbe for a blessing. "Well, what of it?" commented the Maggid. "The Lord sometimes likes to show that He can accomplish a miracle, the same as a rebbe."

Schechter on Ẓaddik-Worship

This "ẓaddik-worship" is probably the aspect of Ḥasidism that was most severely attacked by students of the movement. They were no doubt influenced by the excesses of some ẓaddikim in the middle of the 19th century. There were ẓaddikim who led an unwholesome life of luxury, and even those who, under the pretense of concealing their piety, indulged in dissipation and immorality. Solomon Schechter, in his classical essay on Ḥasidism, blamed ẓaddikism for the "corruption and perversion" of the movement. Schechter charged the later

Ḥasidim with having taken a relatively minor point in the Ba'al Shem Tov's teaching – the honor due to the divine in man – and given it an exaggerated and distorted importance. The unfortunate result, was "an almost idolatrous service of their living leaders."

Schechter maintained that it was the "peculiar doctrine of the Intermediary" that soon became Ḥasidism's distinguishing feature. "By a Chassid was understood not a man who held such and such opinions in theology and religion, but a believer in the Zaddik, and one who sought to attain salvation through the worship of the Zaddik. Every other doctrine of Chassidism was

Left : Solomon Halberstam of Bobov, born in 1908, the present leader of the Bobover Ḥasidim.
Right : Joel Teitelbaum, the Satmarer rebbe.

rapidly pushed into the background and overlooked. Even the grand and fundamental doctrine of Omnipresence in the Creation was veiled by the special presence in the Zaddik. Chassidism became mere Zaddikism. . . ."

Scholem's View

As against this indictment of later Ḥasidism we have the more recent verdict of Gershom Scholem that ẓaddikism was in no sense a corruption of the "pure" Ḥasidism of the Ba'al Shem Tov. "This simon-pure Ḥasidism never existed because anything like it could never have influenced more than a few people. The . . . later development of ẓaddikism was already implicit in the very start of the Ḥasidic movement. As soon as the mystic felt the urge to perpetuate his personal and solitary experience in the life of a community . . . the believer no longer needed the Kabbalah; he turned its mysteries into reality by fastening upon certain traits which the saint, or ẓaddik, whose example he strove to follow, had placed in the center of his relation to God. . . . All this demanded from the first . . . the existence of the ẓaddik or saint as the actual proof of the possibility of living up to the ideal." Scholem is of course not defending "ẓaddik-worship"; he is simply trying to put the phenomenon in the proper historical perspective.

6. FERVOR PLUS REASON

Isaac Leib Peretz, in his heartwarming tale about a Ḥasidic rebbe, "If Not Higher," gives us a vivid definition of a "Litvak." To say that Litvaks are Lithuanian Jews is correct but hardly adequate, Peretz tells us. As far as the Ḥasidim were concerned, the Litvaks were "casuists, intellectual exhibitionists, verbal prestidigitators, dry-hearted, small-spirited, ingenious manipulators of Talmudic texts. . . . Rational and pedantic, they knew only such truths – if such truths there be – that can be demonstrated black on white, deduced from the Talmud and its commentaries, which of course

Shneur Zalman of Lyady (1747-1813), founder of Ḥabad Ḥasidism.

they knew by heart. But of the truths of the heart – and perhaps these are the only truths – they knew nothing."

Shneur Zalman of Lyady

If, in the third generation of the movement, Ḥasidism struck roots in the hostile soil of Lithuania, this was due mainly to the personality and efforts of Shneur Zalman of Lyady (1745-1813), whom we have already had occasion to mention. At the age of twenty, he left his wife with her parents and went to Mezhirech to learn Ḥasidism from the Great Maggid. It is said that he took this step after arriving at the conclusion that he knew "a little about learning but nothing about prayer." How much he actually knew about prayer is unknown, but for learning that is surely an understatement, for at the age of 12 he had been recognized as an *illui* – a child prodigy – and accepted as a colleague and an

Rabbi Menaḥem Mendel Schneersohn, the present Lubavicher rebbe, completing the *mitzvah* of dressing a Torah scroll.

A typical scene in a Ḥasidic *shtibl,* entitled "Study," by Isidor Kaufmann. The rabbi, leaning on a movable lectern or *shtender,* leads an informal study group.

equal by the leading scholars of Vitebsk, where he was then studying. Among the Maggid's disciples Shneur Zalman was known as "the Litvak," but his mastery of talmudic literature was soon recognized, and the Maggid assigned him the task of composing a new and up-to-date *Shulḥan Arukh* (code of Jewish law). *The Litvak*

We have noted that after the Maggid's death in 1772, the leadership of the Ḥasidic movement became diffused. Shneur Zalman not only attracted many devoted disciples of his own, but by 1788 it became apparent that he had created a distinct type of Ḥasidism, which was to become known as "Ḥabad" a name derived from the initial letters of the three highest of the ten *sefirot*, or spheres, to which according to the Kabbalah emanate from God: *ḥokhmah* (wisdom), *binah* (reason), *da'at* (knowledge). In other words reason and intellect were to be reinstated as a way to find God. Before the advent of Shneur Zalman, Ḥasidism had not been based on any system that could *Reason Reinstated*

Chaim Gorr's portrait of the sixth Lubavicher rebbe, Joseph Isaac Schneersohn (1880-1950), a descendant of Shneur Zalman of Lyady, and father-in-law of the present Lubavicher rebbe. The latter, Menaḥem Mendel Schneersohn, is also a descendant of Shneur Zalman through another branch of the family.

Shneur Zalman stressed the need for regular study and unceasing spiritual exercise as the way to find God. This painting by the German artist, Prischenfried, is entitled "The Talmud Scholar." The books which are being studied, however, are clearly not copies of the Talmud, nor is there any reason why the boy should be wearing a *tallit* while he studies.

be studied by regular methods. This he changed with the publication of his *Likkutei Amarim* ("collected sayings"), popularly known as the *Tanya*. A masterly and systematic exposition of Ḥasidism, it was accepted as "the written law of Ḥabad."

Ḥerem and Counter-Ḥerem

Shneur Zalman stressed the necessity for regular study and unceasing spiritual exercise as indispensable for the achievement of lasting results. From this he derived a new ethical concept of the *beinoni* ("the average man"). The ẓaddik he defined as an exceptional type, whose characteristics are inborn and who directs all his spiritual life towards attaining the transition to the Divine. This person is extremely rare, however, and there exists a hiatus between him and the average man that is almost impossible to bridge. The practical Jewish ideal is a different figure, that of the *beinoni*.

The *beinoni* that "every man should aspire to become" is the person who does not manage in the unconscious depths of his soul to achieve complete spiritual identity with the Divine, yet who in his everyday life, as also in his emotions and intellect, strives toward perfection. Whereas the ẓaddik is chosen from birth, the ideal of the *beinoni* can be achieved in practice and is expected of every Jew. In contrast to the Ba'al Shem Tov, Shneur Zalman held that it is not expected of the *beinoni* to transform "alien thoughts"; he is required to turn away from them, to resist evil throughout his life. It is only the ẓaddik that is not forbidden contact with the powers of temptation. Instinctive reverence, like "the hidden love that is in the heart of every Jew from birth," forms the primary basis from which every *beinoni* may advance to higher degrees of perfection. The struggle of the *beinoni* against the evil impulse (*yeẓer ha-ra*) within him is sustained by the fact that "the brain rules the heart from birth" and by perseverence in resort to meditation (*hitbonenut*). One might well conclude that the *beinoni* is now, in fact, not "average" at all but the righteous man who struggles against the evil within him in order to do God's will.

Differs With the Besht

Meditation on the greatness of the Creator, on love and reverence for Him, results in the elevation of the primitive feelings in the sacred soul to a higher degree of "love and rational reverence," Shneur Zalman taught. This does not necessarily imply an intellectual or rationalist approach to adherence to God, but is essentially the propulsion of the hidden emotional life to a degree of full awareness. Similarly, there must be strict adherence to the norms of traditional Jewish ethical behavior, such as punctiliousness in the performance of the *mitzvot*, additional stress on Torah study, and the worship of God in joyousness while repressing melancholy. Attaching particular significance to the role of meditation as a primary means of achieving elevation in the Ḥasidic progression, Shneur Zalman regarded the study of Kabbalah not as a theoretical exercise but essentially as a means of strengthening faith in the Creator and of arousing the heart.

Study of Kabbalah

Shneur Zalman held that the physical world, precisely because it conceals the divine manifestation, is an expression of the highest degree of the divinity ("material creation derives from the divine substance"). From this explanation certain conclusions follow concerning the conduct of man: fulfillment of the practical precepts, precisely because they are materialistic, and study of the Torah, precisely because it is linked with material factors in the world, are higher degrees than theoretical spiritual adhesion to God. Observance of the *mitzvot*, such as Torah study, forms a link – and in fact the only one – of real adhesion to God. It follows that love of God and reverence for Him, and even the feeling of adhesion to Him, are only a means of arousing the soul towards the true adhesion – through Torah study and observance of the *mitzvot*.

Mitzvot as a Link to God

Since the way to God thus depends on essentially the individual's own efforts – on his study, his meditation and his observance of the *mitzvot* – the mediation of the ẓaddik is no longer required. He is no longer an intercessor and miracle worker but a spiritual guide and leader. In practice, however, Shneur Zalman was only partially successful in curbing ẓaddik-worship. Ḥabad Ḥasidim flocked to Lyady in such numbers that he was compelled to issue rules which provided, *inter alia*, that no Ḥasid was to visit the city more than once a year. "I cannot adequately describe," he wrote in a pastoral letter to his fol-

Boys from both Ashkenazi and Sephardi backgrounds studying at the Lubavicher yeshivah at Kefar Ḥabad in Israel. Ḥasidism today is also attracting Jews of Oriental extraction.

lowers in 1793, "the extent to which my very life is embittered by those who come in to me to pour out before me personally their sorrow in detail."

Shneur Zalman has been called the "Maimonides of Ḥasidism." But his synthesis of Ḥasidic fervor and worship with Lithuanian rationality and learning did not have the effect – not during his own lifetime at any rate – of making Ḥasidism any more acceptable to the Mitnaggedim. In fact, the opposite seems to have been the case. The fact that Shneur Zalman's influence had begun to penetrate the strongholds of the Mitnaggedim spurred them to make a last effort to check the spread of Ḥasidism by informing on its leaders to the Russian government. Avigdor ben Joseph Ḥayyim, the rabbi of Pinsk, in 1798 formally accused Shneur Zalman of treason against the state (his dispatch of money to Palestine, for example, was described as "helping the Turkish sultan"). Shneur Zalman was arrested and taken to St. Petersburg for trial, eventually being acquitted and released. But for years afterwards Rabbi Avigdor was referred to in Ḥasidic writings as "Avigdor the wicked," "Avigdor the informer, may his memory be blotted out."

Arrested for Treason

Nor did Shneur Zalman's insistence that there could be no true fear and love of God without intellectual inquiry and effort endear him to other leaders *within* the Ḥasidic camp. Most of the latter preferred the virtue of simple faith in God and in the sages, fearing that intellectual pursuit would lead to heresy. Abraham of Kalisk (1741-1810) who, like Shneur Zalman, had been a disciple of the Maggid of Mezhirech, criticized him not only for his emphasis on intellectual inquiry but also for encouraging the study of the Lurianic Kabbalah and the esoteric teachings of the Ba'al Shem Tov and the Maggid. (Shneur Zalman was equally at home in the Talmud and in the Kabbalah.) Such studies, thought Abraham of Kalisk, were meant only for a chosen few and not for the rank-and-file. To this day, in fact, other Ḥasidic trends tend to look upon the Ḥabad-Lubavich wing as a breed apart.

Opposition From Within

7. BANS AND BOOK-BURNINGS

The anti-Ḥasidic forces, to which we have made a number of passing references, were led by one of the greatest spiritual and intellectual leaders of Jewry in modern times, Elijah, the Gaon of Vilna (1720-97), under whose influence Vilna – "the Jerusalem

The Gaon of Vilna

of Lithuania" – took the lead in the battle against Ḥasidism. To the Gaon, Ḥasidism's ecstasy, the visions seen and the miracles wrought by its leaders, and its enthusiastic way of life were not

A painting of Elijah ben Solomon Zalman (1720-1797), the Gaon of Vilna, and a leader of the anti-Ḥasidic forces.

only delusions but dangerous lies and idolatrous worship of human beings. The Ḥasidic elevation of contemplative prayer and the serving of God in joy over all other obligations, especially over the study of the Torah, seemed to be a complete reversal of the traditional scale of values. The bizarre practice of turning somersaults in prayer, which was followed by a number of the early Ḥasidim as an expression of self-abnegation, was held up to

ridicule, as was Ḥasidic indulgence in alcoholic stimulants and tobacco. Various Ḥasidic changes in the rules governing the knives used in *sheḥitah*, their switch from the Ashkenazi to the Lurianic-Sephardi prayer rite, their encouragement of young men to leave their families for long periods to stay at the court of the ẓaddik, were all anathema to the Mitnaggedim, who saw in the whole process a determined revolt against the established order. Rarely did Ḥasidism's opponents clearly express their real suspicion: that it was a new version of the messianic movements of Shabbetai Ẓevi and Jacob Frank – a suspicion that was the underlying reason for the vehemence of the various *ḥerem* declarations and the polemical works of the Mitnaggedim.

Ḥerem and Counter-Ḥerem

In 1772 the Vilna Jewish community disbanded the *minyan* formed by the Ḥasidim and issued a *ḥerem* against them; Ḥasidic works were burned, and the first anti-Ḥasidic pamphlet, *Zemir Ariẓim ve-Ḥorvot Ẓurim* ("Uprooting of Tyrants and Flinty Swords"), was published. A *ḥerem* against the Ḥasidim was also proclaimed in the city of Brody the same year. The Ḥasidim countered with a *ḥerem* of their own and with burning the *Zemir Ariẓim*. In 1772 and again in 1777 Menaḥem Mendel of Vitebsk and Shneur Zalman of Lyady, the leaders of the Ḥasidic movement in Belorussia, traveled to Vilna to meet Elijah Gaon and demonstrate that the new movement did not conflict with traditional Judaism, but the Gaon refused to see them. After the publication in 1781 of Jacob Joseph of Polonnoye's *Toledot Ya'akov Yosef*, with its criticism of the rabbis of the day, the Gaon intensified his fight against Ḥasidism. (Jacob Joseph denounced the ordinary type of rabbi as "Jewish demons, the equivalent of Satan and the evil inclination itself, all of their Torah studies being for their personal aggrandizement.") Through the Gaon's influence, another harsh *ḥerem* was proclaimed against the Ḥasidim in 1781, and emissaries were sent

Snubbed by the Gaon

Ḥerem (excommunication order) imposed by the rabbis of Cracow on the city's Ḥasidim in 1786.

Isaac Erter (1791-1851) wrote satires against Ḥasidism. He depicted the Ḥasidic world as hypocritical, ignorant and superstitious.

out to rouse the communities against the movement.

They Must Leave Our Communities

"They must leave our communities with their wives and children," the ban declared, "and they should not be given a night's lodging; their *sheḥitah* is forbidden; it is forbidden to do business with them and to intermarry with them, or to assist at their burial." As a result of these bans merchants lost their customers, teachers lost their pupils, and betrothals were broken off. In this period it became the rule among the Mitnaggedim not to allow their children to marry into Ḥasidic families.

Vilna's lead was followed by many other communities. The following circular is typical of the measures that failed to halt

Ḥasidism's progress. It was issued in 1786 by the anti-Ḥasidic community of Shklov, in White Russia:

Insane Worship

> Because of our many sins, worthless and wanton men who call themselves Ḥasidim have deserted the Jewish group and have set up a so-called place of worship for themselves. And thus, as everyone knows, they worship in a most insane fashion following a different ritual which does not conform to the religion of our holy Torah, and they tread a path which our fathers never trod. In addition to this the works of their teachers have, unfortunately, recently been published, and it is obvious to us that all of their writings are opposed to our holy Torah and that they contain misleading interpretations. The exaggerations and stories of miracles that are described in their books are particularly evident and obvious lies, and far be it from us to place any trust in any such exaggerated statements. And behold, as a result of this great misfortune, a fire has been kindled, unfortunately, in the midst of Jewry, and there is a breaking away from the obligations imposed by the Torah.

Caricature of a Brody Ḥasid by J. Pennell the 19th century English artist.

This indictment was followed by a list of rigorous measures that the disseminators of the circular urged all communities to adopt against the Ḥasidim. In addition to proclaiming a day of fasting and public prayer, and declaring meat slaughtered by Ḥasidic *shoḥetim* unfit to eat, the circular proposed the following action:

Rigorous Measures

> All possible measures are to be adopted to put an end to the prayer-meetings of the heretics in all communities, so that they will be deprived of the possibility of common assembly.
>
> Careful watch is to be maintained that no one should study their literature, and search is to be made with this purpose in mind . . . .
>
> No one is to shelter any member of this sect. No member of the above-mentioned sect may bring suit in a Jewish court. No community may permit any one of them to hold a position as cantor or rabbi, and it goes without saying that no one of them may teach our children.
>
> It is to be announced in all communities that any one who knows anything, good or bad, about the Ḥasidim must bring his information to the court.

They Have Sin in Their Hearts

In the 1790s the struggle became even sharper. Around 1794 the Gaon gave instructions that *Ẓavva'at ha-Ribash* ("The Testament of Rabbi Israel Ba'al Shem Tov") should be publicly burned in Vilna. In 1796, the Ḥasidim having spread a rumor that Elijah regretted his stand against the movement, the Gaon replied in a letter sent by special emissaries to the communities of Lithuania and Belorussia: "I will continue to stand on guard, and it is the duty of every believing Jew to repudiate and pursue them with all manner of afflictions and subdue them, because they have sin in their hearts and are like a sore on the body of

Israel." Not infrequently both Ḥasidim and their opponents denounced each other to the secular authorities, leading to the arrest of a number of Ḥasidic leaders and mutual calumnies of a grave nature.

The Criticism of Ḥayyim of Volozhin

It was a disciple of the Gaon of Vilna – Ḥayyim of Volozhin (1749-1821), founder of the renowned Yeshivah of Volozhin – who made the most profound, systematic and scholarly attack on Ḥasidism. In his book *Nefesh ha-Ḥayyim* (1824), in which the term Ḥasid is discreetly omitted, he presents Ḥasidism as a spiritual movement that ignores a cardinal principle in Judaism: where the essence of a *mitzvah*, or its observance, is jeopardized by an idea, the idea must be set aside. Similarly, if new values – lofty though they may be – threaten to come into conflict with tradition, it is the tradition that must be upheld. Unlike most critics of Ḥasidism, Ḥayyim of Volozhin rarely voices an objection to specific Ḥasidic practices: he takes issue on a theoretical basis with fundamental beliefs of Ḥasidism that he regarded as dangerous. Thus, he objects to the centrality in Ḥasidic doctrine of the necessity for "purity of thought," holding that the essence of the Torah and *mitzvot* does not necessarily lie in their being performed with "great *kavvanah* and true *devekut*." Here Ḥayyim of Volozhin points out the conflict between mysticism and the *halakhah*. He emphasizes the dialectic process by which the performance of a *mitzvah* with excessive *kavvanah* leads to the destruction of the *mitzvah*. The very act of fulfilling the *mitzvah* is the fundamental principle, and not the *kavvanah* accompanying its performance. Here he challenges Ḥasidism on a matter of basic principle: performing *mitzvot* "for the sake of heaven," he insists, is not a value in itself.

The Role of Kavvanah

Replying to the Ḥasidic charge that it was common for Talmud scholars to be motivated by considerations of prestige, wealth and fame, Rabbi Ḥayyim held that Torah study even for ulterior motives was not to be despised. Moreover, he rejected the Ḥasidic interpretation of the idea of *Torah li-shemah* ("Torah for its own sake") as meaning that the student should have God in mind when he studies the texts. Such an attempt, he argues, would interfere with the intense concentration required for the mastery of difficult halakhic studies. The student should have a few moments of prayer and devout thoughts before his actual studies and then he should immerse himself in the texts. Yet Rabbi Ḥayyim distinguished between the ideological aspect of the controversy and the communal one. Thus, despite his enormous reverence for the Vilna Gaon (rivaling the loyalty of a Ḥasid to his ẓaddik), he did not sign the ban against the Ḥasidim.

Horodezky's View

According to one student of Ḥasidism, S. A. Horodezky, the rabbis opposed Ḥasidism for the same reason that the Pharisees opposed Jesus. It was not so much the tenets of the new movement that were objectionable, Horodezky maintains, but the supernatural role and exaggerated authority that it assigned to the ẓaddik, who sometimes was made to appear superior to the Torah itself. Horodezky seems to be excessively deprecatory of the role of Ḥasidic theory in arousing opposition, but there can be no doubt that without ẓaddikism Ḥasidism would have found it much easier to gain acceptance.

The Judaizing of Ḥasidism

It should also be kept in mind that in the course of time Ḥasidism divorced itself of some of its more heretical features, thus removing some of the causes of rabbinic opposition. There is much to be said for the view that attributes the healing of the rift between Ḥasidism and Mitnaggedism to the "Judaizing" of Ḥasidism, largely through the work of Ḥabad. The third Lubavicher Rebbe, Rabbi Menaḥem Mendel, even conceded that there had been a solid basis for the Vilna Gaon's fear that the new system "would gradually lead us, step by step, beyond the boundaries set by tradition and Torah law." The fact that the founder of Ḥabad was himself a victim of the persecution of the

Mitnaggedim does not necessarily constitute a refutation of this view.

The Attack by the Haskalah

But it was not only the traditionalists that opposed Ḥasidism: it also was attacked by the leaders of the Haskalah, or Enlightenment, who saw in it nothing but charlatanism, uncouth frenzy and ridiculous superstition. The Maskilim regarded the doctrines and the leaders of Ḥasidism as an obstacle to the modernization of Jewish life, and they satirized the new movement mercilessly. Joseph Perl (1773-1839), a leading figure in the Galician Haskalah who had been attracted to Ḥasidism in his youth, even encouraged the Austrian authorities in Galicia, in an incessant stream of denunciatory notes (only recently discovered and published) which he sent to the officials, to take measures against the Ḥasidim. In the literary sphere he battled against the movement by means of propaganda, parody, and satire. Characteristic is his German book, *On the Character of the Ḥasidic Sect* (1816), in which he condemns Ḥasidic practices and beliefs on the ground that they jeopardize the welfare of the state and mislead innocent believers. He denigrates Ḥasidism by presenting a hostile, often distorted anthology of quotations lifted out of context from Ḥasidic sources. Perl's principal work, *Megalleh Temirin* ("The Revealer of Secrets"; 1819), is the foremost parody against Ḥasidism, and it won immense popularity. It imitates the pious style of Ḥasidic miracle books, so successfully in fact, that some of the faithful are said to have accepted it as one of their own works. Here Perl describes the machinations of the Ḥasidic leaders in their struggle for influence and material gain. In his satire these leaders resort to bribery, intimidation and blackmail against their rivals, whether rabbis or Maskilim. Its character sketches were so true to life that some Ḥasidim are said to have avoided appearing in public for fear of being pointed out as the originals.

Parody and Satire

Ḥasidism was also satirized by Isaac Baer Levinsohn (1788-

1860), one of the founders of the Haskalah in Russia, and Isaac Erter (1791-1851), who together with other young Maskilim had been excommunicated in Lvov in 1816 by Rabbi Jacob Ornstein, the rabbi of the city. Levinsohn, in *Emek Repha'im* ("The Valley of the Dead"), depicts a ẓaddik in hell (and not in heaven where one might have supposed him to have found his final resting place), where he confesses that, lacking both talmudic and secular learning, the only career open to him had been that of a Ḥasidic rabbi. Erter's collected satires, *Ha-Ẓofeh le-Veit Yisrael* ("A Watchman unto the House of Israel"; 1858), portray Ḥasidism as a combination of hypocrisy, ignorance and superstition.

Zweifel Defenc[e of] Ḥasidism

In sharp contrast to the general hostility manifested by Haskalah writers towards Ḥasidism was Eliezer Zweifel's (1815-88) *Shalom al Yisrael* ("Peace to Israel"; 1868-73). In his balanced and informed argument, Zweifel undertook an analysis of fundamental Ḥasidic sayings and teachings, pointing out their significance and underscoring, too, their uniqueness in comparison with Kabbalah. Zweifel's defence of Ḥasidism relates specifically to the early stages of its development. As a Maskil he of course had reservations about the "popular" elements of Ḥasidism and about a number of its social aspects: he criticizes the negative features which emerged in the later period of the movement, particularly the cult of the ẓaddik. The book aroused indignation among the Maskilim, and Jewish censors sympathetic to the Haskalah tried to prevent its publication.

With the appearance of the Haskalah as an enemy common to all Orthodoxy, the bitterness and ferocity of the struggle between Ḥasidism and Mitnaggedim abated, the erstwhile opponents joining hands to stamp out the new threat. However,

Uneasy Co-existence

basic differences between Ḥasidim and Mitnaggedim remained with respect to the ranking of various Jewish values, the place of the ẓaddik in the communal leadership, and the permissibility of certain ecstatic manifestations in the Ḥasidic way of life. Some-

"The Sasover Rebbe," by Zigmunt Menkes (1896 -   ).

Self portrait by Abraham Jacob Shapiro of Dorohobich, who was *admor* of the Grodzisk dynasty from 1922 until his death in 1962.

"Last Prayer," by Samuel Hirschenberg (1865-1908).

times latent sometimes active, these differences never wholly subsided. But owing to the growing conservatism of Ḥasidism, there emerged an uneasy coexistence between them and the Mitnaggedim. By the middle of the 19th century, Ḥasidism prevailed in most communities of the Ukraine, Volhynia, central-Poland, Galicia, and in many areas in Hungary and Belorussia – and the pattern of leadership based on the ẓaddik changed the character of local community leadership. Local leaders and rabbis now became subject to the authority of that ẓaddik whose followers were the most influential Ḥasidic group in a given community. In short, in the conflict between the Ḥasidim and the Mitnaggedim, it was the Ḥasidim who were eventually victorious.

8. THE ẒADDIK WHO TALKED BACK TO GOD

While a common body of doctrine and practice united all ẓaddikim and distinguished them from other Jewish leaders, there were also pronounced differences between one ẓaddik and another. The dispute over "practical ẓaddikism" has been mentioned. Some ẓaddikim encouraged their followers to believe in their miraculous powers; others – "the holy Jew" of Przysucha was one of these – discouraged such belief. Many ẓaddikim advocated and practiced loud prayer, punctuated with groans, sighs and exclamations; others taught that quiet prayer was the best, and Menaḥem Mendel of Warka (1819-68) exemplified this viewpoint so perfectly that he is known as "the silent ẓaddik."

A Carriage and Four

Since the attraction of Ḥasidism depended so much on the charisma of the ẓaddik, it is not surprising that it was unusually rich in distinctive personalities. There was Simḥah Bunem of Przysucha (1765-1827), who was a pharmacist before he became a ẓaddik; there was Israel Friedman of Ruzhin (1797-1858), the rebbe of Sadgora, who lived in princely opulence, surrounded by

1

2

3

4

Members of the Ruzhin dynasty: 1. Israel Friedman of Ruzhin (1797-1858), 2. Dov of Leovo (1827-1876), 3. David Moses of Chortkov (1828-1900), 4. Ḥayyim David Manzon of Brad (1850-1932), 5. Israel of Chortkov (1854-1934), 6. Israel of Husyatin (1856-1949), 7. Shalom Joseph of Melnitza-Podolskaya (died 1927), 8. Moses of Boyan-Cracow (1881-1943), 9. Abraham Jacob of Sadgora (1884-1961), 10. Mordecai Shelomo of Boyan-New York (1891-1971), 11. Aaron of Chernovtsy (died 1941/2), 12. Mordecai Shalom Joseph of Sadgora-Przemzyl (1897-), 13. Isaac Jacob of Husyatin (1900-1968), 14. Jacob Joseph Solomon Halperin of Vaslui (1902-), 15. Isaac of Buhusi (1903-).

6

7

8

9

11

12

13

14

many servants, and who rode in a splendid carriage and four. There was even a woman ẓaddik, the so-called "Maid of Ludomir" (1805-92), who in order to observe the separation of the sexes, would deliver Sabbath discourses to her Ḥasidim from an adjoining room, she herself remaining unseen.

There were many more notable ẓaddikim, but in this brief survey we shall discuss only two of them: Levi Isaac of Berdichev and Menaḥem Mendel of Kotsk.

Intercessor for Israel

Levi Isaac of Berdichev (c. 1740-1810) was known as Israel's *meliẓ yosher* ("advocate" or "intercessor"). One of the intimate circle of pupils of the Maggid of Mezhirech, he stressed the element of joy in Ḥasidism, the principle of *devekut*, and the necessity for fervent prayer to the point of *hitpashetut ha-gashmiyyut* ("divesting oneself of corporeality"). When a man prays fervently "with all his heart and all his soul, his spirit delights because it is elevated from the material world and only the spirit remains." One of the best-loved ẓaddikim, Levi Isaac occasionally traveled with great acclaim throughout the land. Accompanied by his *minyan*, he introduced the people to the joy of fulfilling the commandments, winning many of them over to Ḥasidism.

Nothing But Good

The "Berdichever" became a popular hero in Jewish poetry and fiction, both in Hebrew and in Yiddish. He shared the distress of his people and worked to improve their living conditions. In singing his prayers he addressed the Creator in Yiddish; popular tradition has preserved some of these prayers, e.g., "The Kaddish of Rabbi Levi Isaac." He stressed the good that is in man and always pleaded the cause of the Jews. "No one," he maintained, "has a right to say anything evil about the Jewish people, but only to intercede for them." Like the Ba'al Shem Tov, he took to task those preachers who seemed to take a perverse delight in ruthlessly exposing Jewish shortcomings. Only he who "admonishes the Jewish people gently, elevates their souls and always extols their righteousness is worthy of being their leader."

Many of the tales told of Levi Isaac show his unbounded love for Israel, whose cause he never failed to plead before the Throne of Judgment. Thus when he saw a teamster oiling the wheels of his wagon while wearing his *tallit* and *tefillin*, instead of rebuking

Two pages from the handwritten illuminated manuscript on vellum known as the *siddur* of the rabbi of Ruzhin. It was written in Germany in 1460 and later came into the possession of Rabbi Israel of Ruzhin. Both pages are from the Passover service.

him for sacrilege he exclaimed: "O Lord, what a holy people is Thine! Even when they oil the wheels of their wagons they pray unto Thee in *tallit* and *tefillin*!" Another famous story tells of his seeing a Jew eating in public on the Fast of Av. "Surely you must have forgotten that today is the Ninth of Av," Levi Isaac said to him. "No, I have not forgotten," was the reply. "Then perhaps you are unwell?" continued the rabbi. "No, I am in excellent health." The rabbi lifted his eyes towards heaven and exclaimed: "O Lord, behold how thy Jews love the truth. Even when they transgress Thy commandments they do not stoop to utter falsehoods!"

Unbounded Love for Israel

Listless Prayer

But Levi Isaac also knew how to speak out when the occasion demanded it. Listless prayer was one thing that aroused his ire. Once, after the congregation had finished praying the *Amidah*, he walked over to a group of his Ḥasidim, shook their hands and greeted them with "Shalom Aleikhem." They were puzzled by this ceremoniousness, usually reserved for guests or for Ḥasidim who had been out of town. The rabbi soon explained: "The reason for this salutation is that I could read in your faces when you were reciting the *Amidah* that you did not have in mind the meaning of the prayers but were thinking of the grain market in Odessa and the wool market in Lodz. Now that you have returned from so far a distance, it is only right that I extend you a welcome home."

When Rabbi Abraham of Kalisk wrote him criticizing the views and conduct of Rabbi Shneur Zalman of Lyady, citing in support the testimony against him by certain "men of scholarship, piety and truth," Levi Isaac replied: "I have never seen among them men of scholarship, piety and truth. How can you write about them 'men of truth' when Tzvi Hamar has spoken many falsehoods in my presence; and if he is a scholar, I do not know who is an *am ha-areẓ*." Like Shneur Zalman, Levi Isaac himself had been an object of persecution by the Mitnaggedim, who had driven him out of Pinsk in 1785.

Nor did his overwhelming love for his people blind Levi Isaac to social evils. When he discovered how hard Jewish women were working, from early morning to late at night, preparing Passover *mazzot*, he protested to his congregation: "We are falsely accused by our enemies of using Christian blood in our Passover food. But we do make our *mazzot* with Jewish blood." *Jewish Blood*

Gravestone of Rabbi Levi Isaac of Berdichev (c. 1740-1810).

Yankel the Tailor

Levi Isaac did not hesitate to argue and quarrel with God on behalf of the Jews, addressing Him in language that from anyone else would have been regarded as blasphemy. On Rosh Ha-Shanah and Yom Kippur, the solemn Days of Judgment, he was especially apt to use bold words in defense of his people. One Yom Kippur he called a poor and humble tailor as a "witness," urging him to speak up before the congregation. Said the man, "I, Yankel, am a poor tailor who, to tell the truth, have not been too honest in my work. I have sometimes kept remnants of left-over cloth, and I may have eaten in a non-Jewish home where I was working, without washing my hands. But Thou, O Lord, has taken babies away from their mothers, and mothers from their infants. Let us on this Day of Days be quits. Mayest Thou forgive me as I forgive Thee." Whereupon the Berdichever sighed: "O Yankel, Yankel, why did you let God off so lightly? You might have forced Him to redeem all of Israel."

A Lawsuit on Behalf of Israel

On another Yom Kippur, Levi Isaac suddenly stopped the services and (in his famous Yiddish introduction to the Kaddish, which has been set to music) challenged God as follows:

Good morning to You, Lord of the Universe!
I, Levi Isaac, son of Sarah, of the city of Berdichev,
Have come to You in a lawsuit on behalf of Your people, Israel.
Speak, I demand of You.
What have you against your people Israel?
And why do You oppress Your people, Israel?
Wherein have they sinned to be thus tormented?
And I, Levi Isaac, son of Sarah, of the city of Berdichev, say:
. . . I will not stir from here!
An end there must be to this – it must all stop!
Hallowed and magnified be His great Name.

9. THE REBEL OF KOTSK

Very different in character from Levi Isaac of Berdichev was Menaḥem Mendel of Kotsk (1787-1859), one of the most original Ḥasidic leaders, a rebel and an enigma. Born in Bilgoraj, near Lublin, into a non-Ḥasidic family, he was attracted to the movement in his youth and became a disciple of Jacob Isaac ("the Holy Jew") of Przysucha, and later of Simḥah Bunem of the same city. His teachings, although part of Ḥasidism and in some

"He who learns Torah and is not troubled by it . . . a very scoundrel is better than he." *Ḥeder* in Rzeszow, Poland, before the second World War.

ways continuing its classical lines of thought, are in other respects diametrically opposed to those of the Ba'al Shem Tov.

Ḥasidism Petrified

Zeal of the Prophets

Menaḥem Mendel saw Ḥasidism as petrified, not unlike the Rabbinism it had originally come to shake out of its lethargy. The "throne" of the ẓaddik was bequeathed from father to son, and Ḥasidim did not comprehend the nature of the movement, most of them seeing in it little more than the miraculous powers of the ẓaddik, who could help them ease the burdens of this world. The "Kotzker" proposed to change all this. While the Besht emphasized love, joy and compassion for this world, Menaḥem Mendel demanded constant tension and an unmitigated militancy in the service of God. The furious zeal of the prophets of old came back to life in Kotzk. Other rebbes soothed; the Kotzker scathed. "He who learns the Torah," he said, "and is not troubled by it, who sins and forgives himself, who prays today because he prayed yesterday – a very scoundrel is better than he."

Like his master, "the Holy Jew," the Kotzker held that only by utterly despising the concerns of this world could man hope to serve God properly. But he carried this view further, even defining a Ḥasid as "one who discards this world as worthless." As far as he was concerned, "the entire world is not worth even a single sigh." And there was nothing in the world for the sake of which it was worth becoming obligated to a fellow man. His kind of Ḥasid was one who, no matter what was involved, asked himself, "And what do I want this for?" Commenting on the verse,

Despite Menaḥem Mendel's unconventional behavior, the impact he made on Ḥasidism survived. The Ḥasidim of Gur are his spiritual heirs: here some are depicted in their Sabbath dress and distinctive fur hats (*spodeks*).

"Only take heed to thyself, and keep thy soul diligently . . ." he said that the word "only" (*rak*) always implies the exclusion of something; hence the verse should be understood as saying: "Take little heed to thy body and much heed to thy soul." Possibly with tongue in cheek, Menaḥem Mendel went so far as to say that the Seventh Commandment could be taken to apply to sexual relations with one's own wife. But the fact is that he encouraged his young disciples to leave their wives and children and study Torah with him for months on end. And he himself avoided conjugal relations with his first wife for 25 years. It was not that there was anything intrinsically evil in marital relations, they simply interfered with dedicating one's life to the service of God.

Quality Not Quantity

Such teachings could hardly be expected to have a mass appeal. But Menaḥem Mendel was not interested in numbers. Whereas classical Ḥasidism tried to reach all the Jews, the Kotzker was

Reb Israel Alter, the previous rebbe of Gur, who died in 1948, with some of his Ḥasidim. He is joking with the photographer and postures as if to box the camera.

interested only in the select, the few. Thousands of Ḥasidim flocked to Kotzk from all over Poland, even from the western province of Posen and from Lithuania, in order to see and hear the ẓaddik. But Menaḥem Mendel saw in this very popularity a sign that he had deteriorated. For his aim had been to lead a hundred or so dedicated young men "who would stand on the rooftops and reach the plane of the prophets." To guide such a serious-minded group in a life of Torah and faith – that was a goal worth striving for! Of one rebbe he was told about who allegedly had the power to work miracles his dry comment was: "I would like to know if he is able to perform the miracle of making one real Ḥasid." It had been his hope, he once said, "to have a small number of disciples, but all of whom would be fire. Instead, many came and turned me into water."

Fire and Water

Harsh to Suppliants

Towards the Ḥasidim who came to him for his blessing or advice on mundane matters – whether it had to do with making a living or finding a good match for a daughter whose time had come – he could be harsh and contemptuous. To barren women who begged for his prayer he was apt to reply in the words of the Patriarch Jacob when Rachel complained that she had borne no children: "Am I in God's stead?" When one Ḥasid came and told him how difficult it was for him to make a living and begged for his intercession, Menaḥem Mendel suggested that he pray for himself. The Ḥasid replied that he did not know how to pray to the Great and Awesome King, whereupon the rabbi dismissed him by saying, "In that case, you have a much more serious problem than one of livelihood." In another case, when he was urged to pray on behalf of a pious Ḥasid who had lost his fortune, he answered: "If he really is a Ḥasid and a God-fearing man, he lacks nothing."

One of the Kotzker's basic teachings was that there was no place for formalism or rote either in prayer or in the performance of *mitzvot*. Each day a man must try to find the truth as if he had not known it before. Prayer must come from the heart;

without the proper *kavvanah* prayer was a sham. This was orthodox Ḥasidic doctrine, and we have already seen that many Ḥasidim delayed their prayers beyond the time prescribed in the *Shulḥan Arukh*. But the Kotzker was radical even by Ḥasidic standards, and there were Ḥasidim in Kotzk who would say the Morning Prayer in the evening and the Afternoon Prayer at midnight. Similarly, Menaḥem Mendel taught that the outward form of a *mitzvah* was less important than its inward meaning. "The prohibition against the making of idols includes within itself the prohibition against making idols out of the *mitzvot*." And while Menaḥem Mendel – like Shneur Zalman of Lyady – emphasized the importance of Torah study, here too he taught that this was not an end in itself. The ultimate purpose of such study was to learn a way of life. To a brilliant student who informed him that he had learned the entire Talmud, Menaḥem Mendel put the question: "And what did the Talmud teach you?"

Be Yourself!

Sham, pretense, conformity – these were grievous sins in the eyes of the Rabbi of Kotzk. "Thou shalt not steal" certainly did not mean that one should not steal from others – that was obvious. It meant that one should not steal from oneself. To thine own self be true. It was the duty of every man to seek within himself his particular way in the service of God. It was even wrong for a Ḥasid to imitate the way of his rebbe, for then his own way would be lost – and maybe that way would have brought about the redemption. "If I am I," said the Rabbi of Kotzk, "Because I am I, and you are you because you are you, then I am I and you are you. But if I am I because you are you, and you are you because I am I, then I am not I and you are not you."

This accent on individualism was a hallmark of the entire Przysucha-Kotzk school of Ḥasidism. The following anecdote involving Ḥanokh of Aleksandrow who, together with Menaḥem Mendel was a disciple of Simḥah Bunim of Przysucha and who later became a disciple of Menaḥem Mendel, speaks for itself:

Today a subculture of Ḥasidism has developed and become popular among "hippie" youth. Shlomo Carlebach (with the guitar), a leader of the movement, is pictured here singing and playing at a wedding on Mount Zion, Jerusalem, in 1970.

Simḥah Bunim and Ḥanokh

When Ḥanokh was Simḥah Bunim's disciple it was his duty to act as congregational reader of the Morning Prayer in a house adjoining that of his teacher. Now he was in the habit of praying with vehement gestures and loud cries, quite differently from Rabbi Bunim, who spoke with his characteristic composure even when he conducted the services for the congregation. Once young Ḥanokh was praying when the rabbi entered the room, and he immediately lowered his voice and stopped gesturing. But hardly had he done this, when he reflected and said in his soul: "I am after all not concerned with the rabbi; I am standing before God! " And instantly he resumed his stormy manner of praying. After the service Rabbi Bunim summoned him. "Ḥanokh," he said to him, "today I took pleasure in your praying."

The Mysterious Friday Night

The way to the truth is a tortuous one, Menaḥem Mendel taught, and this was no better exemplified than in his own tortured life. A rebellious and fiery spirit, he consumed himself with his own fire. The climax came one Friday night in 1840, a night that is still enveloped in mystery in the annals of Ḥasidism. Hundreds of his Ḥasidim waited for hours that night for him to recite *Kiddush* and begin the Sabbath meal. But he remained closeted in his room. It was midnight when he finally made his appearance. Accounts differ as to what happened thereafter. It seems that when he was handed the *Kiddush* cup he cast it away. Some say that at this point he shouted, "There is no Judgment and there is no Judge!" Others assert that he cried out: "I demand justice. Have we not suffered enough? Why are you afraid, you flatterers and liars? Get out of here and leave me alone." It is also said that he touched the candlestick and thus ostentatiously sinned against the law of the Sabbath.

Some of his disciples left Kotzk at the close of the Sabbath never to return. Others remained faithful to him despite his blasphemous outburst until his death 19 years later. But during that period Menaḥem Mendel locked himself in his room. Food was passed to him through a window, and only on rare occasions did he open the door and make a brief appearance.

Despite the cloud these final years cast over Menaḥem Mendel's life, the spiritual impact of Kotzk and the revolution it wrought in Ḥasidic life and thought continued to be expressed in the fiery approach to Torah and in the marked restlessness of the Ḥasidic mind, particularly in its manifestations among Polish Jews. For although Menaḥem Mendel of Kotzk did not found a dynasty, his Ḥasidic approach was to a great extent carried on by the ẓaddikim of Gur.

10. THE ḤASIDIC LIFE

At the Court of the Ẓaddik

Since the mediation of the ẓaddik played such a basic role in Ḥasidism, it is easy to understand why it was so imperative for the Ḥasid to visit the ẓaddik's court periodically. For the individual Ḥasid, these visits were both a pilgrimage and an opportunity to be reunited with the brotherhood gathered at the court. The Ḥasid journeyed to his ẓaddik's court at least for the High Holidays (usually leaving his family behind), but each week dozens, or even hundreds, of Ḥasidim would visit the rebbe's court to spend a Sabbath in his shadow. Once there, one of the Ḥasid's first acts was to call on the *gabbai* (the rebbe's assistant) and request him to write up a *kvitl*, a short note stating the nature of his problem or request. An interview would then be

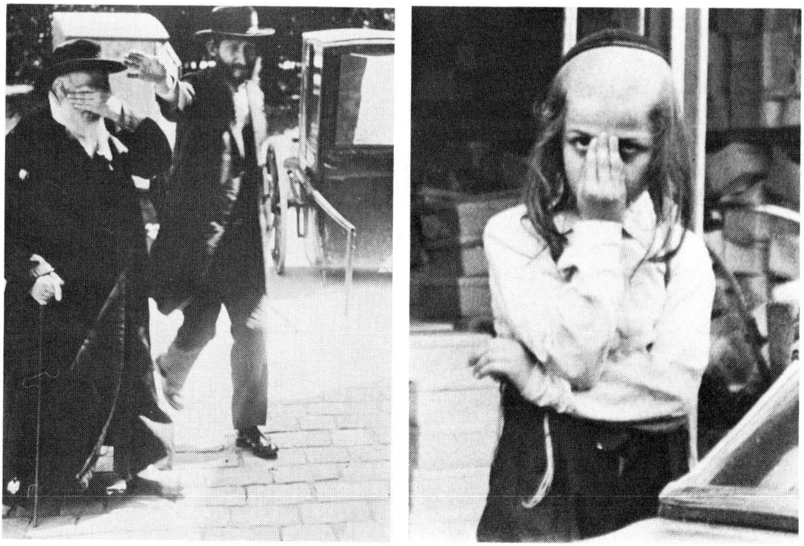

Many Ḥasidim object to being photographed.

arranged with the rebbe, who would give the desired blessing or advice. He might suggest a cure for a sickness, approve or disapprove of a projected business venture, express an opinion about a match the suppliant was considering for his son or daughter. Sometimes the rebbe himself would act as matchmaker, suggesting that Reb Yossel's son marry Reb Gershon's daughter. And for the faithful Ḥasid the rebbe's opinion was law.

A *tish* of the Boyaner Ḥasidim. The rebbe, Rabbi Fridman, blesses the wine and food before distributing the remaining portion *(shirayim)* among his followers.

The Rebbe Never Promise

"The Rebbe himself never promised miracles," one Ḥasid relates. "He only wished that something would happen and said, 'God will help.' But he never promised that a miracle would happen to anyone. It was the people, his followers, who believed that he could work miracles."

In the courts of most rebbes, it was taken for granted that the *kvitl* would be accompanied by a *pidyon*, or monetary contribution, and one commensurate with the suppliant's economic status. The money went towards the upkeep of the rebbe and his court, and was also used to provide for the needs of the poor in the Ḥasidic community. During the High Holidays it was not unusual for a prominent rebbe to be visited by several thousand Ḥasidim. When the Ḥasidim of Gur made their annual pilgrimage to their leader, the Polish railways put on additional trains to accommodate them. But Ḥasidim who could not raise the fare

Holiday Pilgrimage

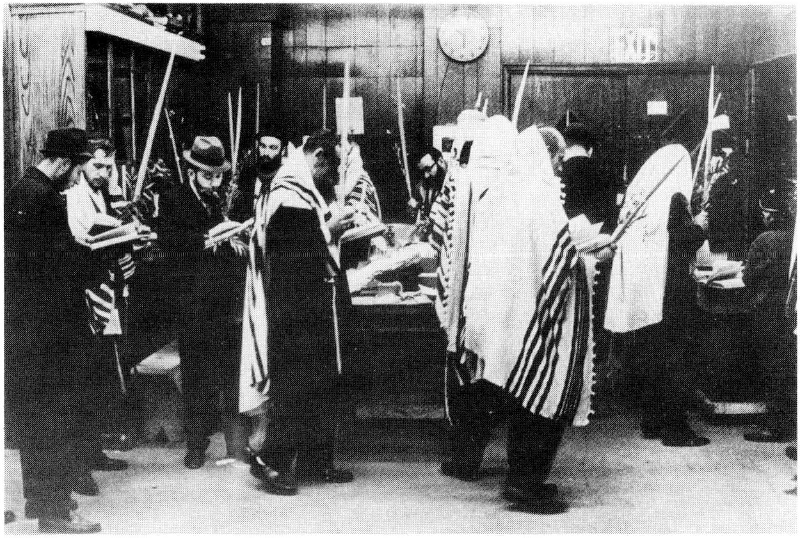

Modern Ḥasidic *shtibl* during the festival of Sukkot. Prayer is informal and individual, and the room is unadorned and austere.

would go to their rebbe by foot, even if this meant walking for weeks.

All Ḥasidic leadership is characterized by an extraordinary magnetism. The ẓaddik is believed in, devoutly admired and obediently followed. From the end of the third generation of Ḥasidism, a dynastic style of leadership often developed, with generation after generation of each dynasty of ẓaddikim following its own *derekh* – its own specific interpretation of the

Wedding of Jonathan Twersky of Tolnoe (born 1906), who stands fourth from the right. To the left of him is Moses Langer of Strettin, his father-in-law, and to the right, his father David Mordecai Twersky (1888-1957).

Ḥasidic way of life. But always there is the obligation of the ẓaddik to participate in the life of his people, listen to their troubles, and try to help them. The ẓaddik is a mystic who employs his power within the social community and for its sake. In the eyes of his Ḥasidim he is a wonder-healer and miracle-worker, a father confessor, a master psychologist, a moral instructor and a practical adviser all in one.

The Third Meal

Surrounded by his followers, the ẓaddik expounds his Ḥasidic teaching at his table ("*der tish*" in Ḥasidic parlance), generally during the third meal on the Sabbath (*se'udah shelishit*). Fish, which has figured in Jewish mysticism since the time of the Talmud, is always eaten, usually in the form of herring. This meal was not a Ḥasidic innovation, but the Ḥasidim vested it with new meaning, transforming it into a celebration of the intimacy between the rebbe and his community. The rebbe is regarded as the ladder between heaven and earth, his mystic contemplation linking him with God, and his concern for the people and his leadership of love tying him to the earth.

Song and Dance

Ḥasidism's insistence on joy (*simḥah*) as the prime factor in the good Jewish life and the essential element of divine worship accounts for its employment of dance and song as expressions of piety and group cohesion, whether in *shtiblekh* (see page 93) in the individual community or when united at the ẓaddik's court and table. Some ẓaddikim ranked music and singing even higher than explicit prayer for the purpose of achieving *devekut*. Since the typical Ḥasidic *niggun*, or tune, is sung without words (with frequent use of carrier syllables such as *Ah, Ay, Oy, Hey, Bam,*

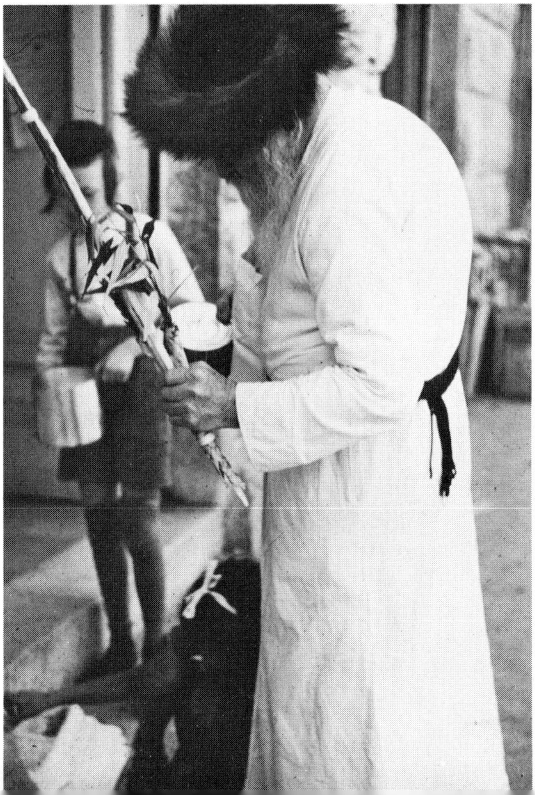

Ḥasid in the traditional dress of the old community of Jerusalem during the festival of Sukkot. The pot in his right hand most probably contains the *etrog*.

Ya-ba-bam, etc.), this predominance of the melodic over the textual aspect may well be directly linked with this doctrine. Ḥasidic dance assumed the form of the circle, symbolic of the Ḥasidic philosophy that "every one is equal, each one being a link in the chain, the circle having no front or rear, no beginning or ending."

The Custom of Shirayim

Another Ḥasidic custom that contributes to the closeness of the Ḥasidic group – though it is likely to repel the outsider – is that of rushing to the rebbe's table to obtain a morsel of the remnants (*shirayim*) of the food he has touched. This may be at the *se'udah shelishit* or at some festive occasion. A recent writer, not unsympathetic, gives the following description of the

Three Ḥasidim examine an *etrog* (citron) carefully, to ensure that it is whole and perfect, and meets the requirements of this *mitzvah* of the Sukkot festival.

custom: "Then the rebbe took a morsel of fish from the plate, ate it, and pushed the plate aside. Immediately, there was bedlam. The Ḥasidim, who a moment before had been frozen against the wall, sprang toward the plate and struggled over it like a pack of famished animals." The Ḥasid, however, has no doubt that if he eats of food that the ẓaddik has blessed he is ensured of both earthly and eternal bliss.

Prayer Rite

From its beginnings Ḥasidism developed its own prayer rite. The Ḥasidic rite, though called *Nusaḥ Sepharad*, is actually not identical with the Sephardi rite; it contains elements of the Polish Ashkenazi rite, changes made by Rabbi Isaac Luria ("Ha-Ari") and the Sephardi rite of the Land of Israel. The result is a patchwork and was a source of considerable confusion; there are even many differences between the various Ḥasidic prayer books. The Ḥasidim downgraded the formality of the synagogue service, stressing in its stead the fervor and excitement that should accompany prayer: their service involves singing, shaking, clapping and body movements.

The Ḥasidic Shtibl

In the first generation of Ḥasidism, while it was still a minority group in most communities and under bitter attack, the Ḥasidim opened small prayer houses of their own, called *shtiblekh* (singular *shtibl*, "small room"), a name used to this day. In the second generation of Ḥasidism, Jacob Joseph of Polonnoye gave a positive reason for praying separately: to improve the nature of the worship. For Jacob Joseph found that in the typical synagogue prayers were rushed through, mechanically, without *kavvanah*; the *ḥazzan* was overly concerned with impressing the congregation, the rich were looking for honor, and the people showed no respect for the house of worship. "He who wants to be holy should set himself apart to pray in a *minyan* of his own, since it is not possible to pray with a congregation which performs the *mitzvot* by rote." The *shtiblekh* were devoid of elaborate furnishings and decorations; in fact they were more of the *bet ha-midrash* type, being places for meetings and study as well as for prayer. Communal meals, particularly the *se'udah shelishit* were held there. The Ḥasidic synagogue did away with salaried officiants; members of the congregation led the prayers themselves and generally the whole atmosphere was very informal. By and large, pews were replaced by tables and benches, and the internal appearance was much more austere than that of the regular synagogue.

Ideal and Practice

Unfortunately, practice did not always rise to the heights of principle, and somewhere along the line the high purpose that had given rise to the *shtibl* was forgotten and it was almost impossible to find in many of them any trace of the awe that one associates with prayer. Perhaps the Ḥasidim were simply too much at home with God. (Herbert Weiner has called attention to the gap between "Buber and Belz" – between Ḥasidism's lofty teachings that so enchanted the philosopher of "I and Thou" and the reality of Ḥasidism in the flesh.)

The memory of past ẓaddikim and the image of living ones are shaped and kept alive through the Ḥasidic tale (*ma'aseh*), which is recounted as an act of homage to the living link between the Ḥasid and God. These tales embody the sayings of the Ba'al Shem Tov and other Ḥasidic leaders, especially Levi Isaac of Berdichev, Naḥman of Bratslav and Menaḥem Mendel of Kotzk. The ecstatic prayer of the ẓaddik – for the most part when reciting the Song of Songs or the *Lekhu Nerannenah* prayer on Sabbath eve – figures frequently in Ḥasidic tales.

Conservative Dress

One of the areas in which Ḥasidism strenuously opposed innovation was that of dress. In the Middle Ages, the imitation of gentile garb had been regarded as *ḥukkat ha-goi* ("customs of the gentiles") and the Jewish minority's retention of its distinctive habits of dress undoubtedly contributed to its survival. It was an easy step from that to turning the Jewish garb worn in Eastern Europe into an emblem of allegiance to traditional Judaism, and

Example 2

= 36 –40
Vald vald vi groys bis - te, royz royz vi vayt bis- te.
Volt der vald nisht a-zoy groys ge-ven, volt di
royz nisht a-zoy vayt ge- ven. Gu-les, gu-les vi
groys bis - te shkhi-ne shkhi-ne vi vayt bis - te.
Volt der gu-les nisht a-zoy groys ge - ven, volt di
shkhi- ne nisht a - zoy vayt ge - ven

Some ẓaddikim ranked music and singing even higher than explicit prayer for achieving *devekut*. This Ḥasidic Yiddish song, *Vald Vald*, is attributed to Rabbi Isaac of Kalov who probably took the melody from a shepherd's love song.

here the Ḥasidim were even more conservative than the Mitnaggedim.

Ḥasidim generally grow their beards long and cultivate earlocks (*pe'ot*; Yiddish, *peyis*). They wear a wide-brimmed black hat, which on the Sabbath may be replaced by the fur-trimmed *shtreimel*. Ties are not customary. Shoes are black, stockings usually white. During prayer a black silk girdle (*gartel*) will be tied around the waist – to separate the animal part of man's body from the upper, distinctly human part. One American Ḥasid gives the following explanation for the earlocks, the beard, the distinctive dress: "After all, if we go dressed like this, there are certain places we can't go to, and things we can't do. It's like a safety belt in the car. It helps prevent accidents."

Women and Ḥasidism

A Ḥasid – even today – avoids looking at women. If he must talk to a woman he will face sideways. On no account will he shake hands with a woman, however. But sometimes even Ḥasidism makes concessions to the demands of modern life. One Ḥasid in Jerusalem who works in a government office has adopted the following compromise: he speaks to the women in the office during work but has explained to them that he cannot talk to them should they happen to meet on the street. Some occupations are avoided altogether as being incompatible with the Ḥasidic way of life. Thus a dentist who became a Ḥasid gave up his profession because it required him "to look into women's mouths."

Enthusiasts of Ḥasidism, such as S. A. Horodezky, assert that the movement gave the woman an honored position she had never enjoyed before, even "complete equality" in religious life. She too went to visit the ẓaddik, even by herself, handed in her *kvitl*, and unburdened herself of her spiritual and material problems. Sometimes she would drag her husband along with her to the ẓaddik. If there was a falling out between husband and wife, all they had to do was go to the ẓaddik and one word from him was enough to restore harmony. Horodezky does not stop here. The woman Ḥasid, he says, unlike her busy husband, always found time to read the writings of the ẓaddikim and to meditate over them, to increase her knowledge, and thus also to influence her husband.

This is obviously an idealized picture of the Ḥasidic woman. In *Shivḥei ha-Besht* a Ḥasid would go to the Ba'al Shem Tov for an amulet and give him money even when his wife gave birth to a girl. In the Ḥasidic *shtibl* the women sit in a thickly screened balcony or even in a separate room. The young disciples of Menaḥem Mendel of Kotzk were not the only Ḥasidim who left their wives for long periods to study with their ẓaddik, despite the wife's tears and her parents' pleading. It is true that Adel, the Besht's daughter, figures in many Ḥasidic legends and was believed to be endowed with Divine Inspiration. And that there was once a woman ẓaddik, the Maid of Ludomir. But two swallows do not make a summer, and even Rabbinism had its Beruryah, the wife of Rabbi Meir, whose views on halakhic matters were seriously reckoned with by her second-century contemporaries. It is difficult not to accept the verdict that "the Ḥasidic congregation was a man's world; in it, there was no place for women."

11. SATMAR, LUBAVICH – AND IN BETWEEN

Although the Holocaust struck the Ḥasidic community more severely than any other part of Jewry, many of the surviving Ḥasidic rebbes succeeded in re-establishing their "courts" in Israel or the United States. A brief description of four of the leading dynasties today – Belz, Gur, Satmar, and Lubavich – will give some notion of the tremendous variety the Ḥasidic movement has managed to encompass within it.

Belz – Normative Ḥasidism

Belzer Ḥasidim may be taken as the "typical" or "classical" type, and practically all we have said about the Ḥasidic way of life

Jerusalemites in the Mea Shearim quarter of Jerusalem. Both Ḥasidim and Mitnaggedim live here but although seven or eight generations have passed since the initial controversy between the two groups, they still maintain separate schools, yeshivot and prayer houses. Note the banner across the street exhorting women to dress modestly.

applies to them without qualification. The Morning Prayer at Belz was delayed until noon, and the conclusion of the Sabbath celebrated around midnight. The founder of the dynasty was Shalom Roke'aḥ (1799-1855), of whose miracle-working many legends are told. Belz – a small town 40 miles north of Lvov – soon became the center of Galician Ḥasidism. Shalom's son Joshua (1825-94) had tens of thousands of followers, in Galicia, Poland and Hungary. Hundreds of them assembled at the rebbe's court each week, and on Rosh Ha-Shanah some 5,000 Ḥasidim would throng to Belz. Joshua was one of the leading opponents of the Haskalah and the Belz ẓaddikim in general adopted an extreme stand, resisting every new idea that emanated from non-Orthodox circles. Jewish traditional dress, for example, was a dogma among the Belzer Ḥasidim, and the adoption of the styles of modern Europe by the Sadeger-Rizhin court evoked Belz's deep antagonism. Joshua's successor, Issachar Dov (1845-1927), a contemporary of Theodor Herzl, strongly opposed Zionism in any form, but his son and successor, Aaron (1880-1957) found refuge in Palestine in 1944 after losing many members of his family in the Holocaust. Here he revised Belz's traditional anti-Zionism and directed his followers to support Agudat Israel. He was succeeded by his nephew, Issachar Dov (1948-), whose marriage in Benei Berak in 1965 (to the granddaughter of the Vishnitzer Rebbe) drew 30,000 guests from all over the world.

Shalom's Miracles

Gur in Poland

In Poland, the dynasty of Gur (Yiddish: Ger; a town about 5 miles from Warsaw) was as celebrated as was that of Belz in Galicia. And, like Belz, its center moved to the Land of Israel as a result of the Holocaust, and most Gerer Ḥasidim now live in Israel. Gur Ḥasidism is based primarily on the Ḥasidic trend developed by "the Holy Jew" of Przysucha and Menaḥem Mendel of Kotzk, and it was the Jew of a scholarly bent that was attracted to its combination of rabbinic learning and Ḥasidic warmth and simplicity. The founder of the dynasty was Isaac Meir Alter (1789-1866) who, after the death of Menaḥem Mendel in 1859, was acknowledged by the majority of the Kotzk Ḥasidim as their rebbe. His novellae on Talmud tractates and the *Shulḥan Arukh*, entitled *Ḥiddushei ha-Rim* (1875) became basic

Issachar Dov (left), the present Belzer rebbe, with his father-in-law (center) Ḥayyim Meir Hager of Vizhnitz, at the Western Wall.

texts for study in the yeshivot. Unlike the Przysucha-Kotzk ẓaddikim, "the Rim" did not withdraw from contact with the masses, but like them he evinced vehement antagonism to miracle working. "If a Ḥasid's motive [for making a pilgrimage] is livelihood, healing or miracle working," he announced shortly after being recognized as a ẓaddik, "he should not come to Gur." None of the Gur ẓaddikim accepted gifts from their followers,

Gifts Rejected

The present rebbe of Gur, Israel Alter, in Jerusalem. The Gur dynasty originated in Poland in the 1850s, and in 1940 moved to Jerusalem where it is now centered.

even in the form of *pidyon*. It was due to the influence of the third rebbe of Gur, Judah Aryeh Leib Alter (1847-1905) that Ḥasidism in Poland dissociated itself from Zionism. But his son, Abraham Mordecai Alter (1866-1948), the last of the dynasty in Poland, influenced thousands of his followers to settle in the Land of Israel. He was one of the founders of Agudat Israel, and under his leadership Gur Ḥasidism reached the height of its

Joel Teitelbaum of Satmar, born 1887, a vigorous opponent of Zionism and of the State of Israel.

influence. He restored the recitation of morning prayer to the regular time and introduced a break during the Sabbath service for public study. He escaped from Gur to Warsaw at the outbreak of World War II, and reached Palestine in 1940. His son, Israel Alter (1892-) succeeded him as rebbe of Gur upon his death in 1948, at the height of the siege of Jerusalem.

Satmar in New York

A Ghetto within Ḥasidism

The largest group of Ḥasidim in New York is the Satmarer, the followers of Joel(ish) Teitelbaum of Satmar (1888-). He is the fifth in a dynasty founded by Moses ben Ẓevi of Ujhely (1759-1841), who was one of the first to spread Ḥasidism in the northern and central districts of Hungary. Because of its intolerant attitude toward other Ḥasidic groups, Satmar has been described as a ghetto within Ḥasidism. In their stronghold in the Williamsburg section of Brooklyn, the Satmarer Ḥasidim today dress much the same as their forbears in Hungary at the turn of the century. The men's earlocks are usually worn so that they are clearly visible, and the married women clip their hair very close to the scalp. Their goal is to maintain their social and intellectual isolation, and they make every effort to protect their children from contamination by the surrounding culture. The Satmarer Rebbe is notorious for his vehement stand and aggressive propaganda against Zionism and the State of Israel, which he maintains have delayed the coming of the Messiah and resulted in all the troubles affecting the Jewish people in the 20th century, including the Holocaust. He holds that a secular-democratic state is inconsistent with the *halakhah*, and that a Jew who lives in the Land of Israel and does not observe the *mitzvot* defiles the land. He has forbidden his followers in Israel to vote in Knesset elections, to visit the Western Wall or to make use of the

Joel Teitelbaum of Satmar while visiting Israel. He is being protected from the crowds by the Israeli police.

country's courts or legal system. For a period, the ultra-Orthodox Natorei Karta community in Jerusalem recognized Joel Teitelbaum as its rabbi. When he visited Israel in 1959 he travelled in a Turkish boat to Haifa and thence to Jerusalem in a special train chartered by Natorei Karta, for which they printed special tickets without the hated Israel insignia. But Satmar's opposition to Israel is not always expressed so passively. The opening of a mixed swimming pool (i.e., where men and women would swim at the same time) in Jerusalem in 1958 led the Satmar group to stage a picketline demonstration at the White House against the "Unheard Brutality of Israel Zionist Police." And Satmarer Ḥasidim so harrassed Jewish leaders in Williamsburg with whom they do not see eye to eye (e.g., telephoning them all through the night, insulting their wives on the street) that at least one of them, an Orthodox rabbi active in the Mizrachi, was forced to move from the neighborhood. It is not easy to find here any trace of the doctrine of love taught by the Ba'al Shem Tov.

Lubavich – The Largest Ḥasidic Group

At the other end of the Ḥasidic spectrum in their attitude towards both the State of Israel and Jews from other camps are the Lubavicher-Ḥabad Ḥasidim whose estimated 250,000 adherents make them the largest Ḥasidic group in the world. We have already described the founding of Ḥabad by Shneur Zalman of Lyady (see page 56). "Lubavich" comes from the Belorussian townlet of that name which became the center of Ḥabad under the leadership of Shneur Zalman's son, Dov Baer (1773-1827). Today Ḥabad is probably the best organized and most dedicated Jewish religious organization in the world. Ḥabad is represented on all continents; the hub of its empire is at 770 Eastern Parkway, in the Crown Heights section of Brooklyn, New York, and there is a large branch in Israel centered at Kefar Ḥabad, near Lydda. The present rebbe, the seventh in the dynasty, is

Menaḥem Mendel Schneershohn. Born in the Russian town Niloaev in 1902, he settled in the United States in 1941, after having studied mathematics and engineering at the Sorbonne. A son-in-law of the sixth Ḥabad Rebbe, he was called upon to assume the leadership in 1950, at the age of 48. Under his direction the influence of Lubavich spread far beyond the Ḥasidic community and penetrated the mainstream of Jewish life in many parts of the world. In theory, the Ḥabad Ḥasid is too sophisticated to expect miracles from his ẓaddik; he looks to him only for spiritual guidance. Nevertheless, the present Rebbe is said to have cured a man of cancer by placing his hand on the man's side and saying *"Si'z gornisht"* ("It's nothing"). A more recent miracle is recounted by the chairman of the Kefar Ḥabad

Studied at the Sorbonne

Menaḥem Mendel Schneersohn, the present Lubavicher rebbe, shown at the age of three.

The late Lubavicher rebbe, Joseph Isaac Schneersohn (1880-1950; left) playing chess with his son-in-law, the present rebbe, Menaḥem Mendel Schneersohn (born 1902).

village council, who spent the High Holidays of 1973 with the Lubavicher Rebbe in Brooklyn. Before his return to Israel the Rebbe gave him a bottle of brandy to take to Zafriyyah, a village near Kefar Ḥabad. When he got there he learned that one of the boys of the village had been seriously wounded in the Yom Kippur War and was lying unconscious in a hospital. It occurred to him that the Rebbe may have had this boy in mind. He went to the hospital, and there he learned that the soldier's watch had stopped when he was hit by a missile, so that the exact time of the incident was known. This turned out to be the very moment that the Rebbe had handed him the bottle of brandy. He told the story to the doctor, who agreed to give the boy a few drops from the bottle. No sooner had he done so than the boy opened his eyes, fully conscious.

A Mission to Jews by Jews

The uniqueness of Ḥabad lies in the fact that it tries to reach other Jews and, if not to make "Ḥabadniks" out of them, at least to draw them a little closer to Orthodoxy. Indeed, in one of its publications, it describes itself as "a mission to Jews by Jews." (In Chaim Potok's recent novel, *My Name is Asher Lev*, the name "Ladover" is a thin disguise for Lubavich.) Ḥabad representatives make regular visits to college campuses and military camps, they conduct a once-a-month kindergarten for a small number of Jewish children who live miles away from the nearest synagogue or Talmud Torah school, and they will even send a *mohel* to circumcise a child on a remote Caribbean island. Ḥabad has developed a widespread network of schools, and it has prepared textbooks for Jewish children who are released from public school one afternoon a week in order to receive religious instruction. In Jerusalem, the tourist visiting the Western Wall is likely to be approached by a Ḥabad Ḥasid with a pair of *tefillin* in his hand, suggesting that he put them on then and there.

12. CONTINUITY OR REVOLT ?

Ḥasidism's Place in Jewish History

Still an unsettled question is the place to be assigned to Ḥasidism in the mosaic of Jewish history.

Buber's Interpretation

Martin Buber (1878-1965) regarded the Ḥasidic teaching as the most powerful and unique phenomenon produced by the Diaspora. Deeply stirred by the religious message of Ḥasidism he undertook to convey that message to the world. From his existentialist teachings, Buber utilized the principle of dialogue as a criterion for understanding the essence of Ḥasidism, which he saw as giving support to the direct encounter, active and creative, between man and the world surrounding him. According to Buber, the dialogue of encounter reveals the reality of God: the cosmos is potentially holy, the encounter with man makes it actually holy. The origin of this fundamental concept, which he called pan-sacramentalism, Buber sought to locate in the Ḥasidic doctrine of the worship of God through the corporeal and worldly dimensions of man's being. The revival of Judaism that found expression in Ḥasidism was seen by Buber as a fresh and living religious phenomenon, but also as a process of social and communal consolidation of novel educational importance.

He believed that the ẓaddikim gave expression to this new educational and religious meaning, for every ẓaddik represented a special experience acquired as a result of the encounter through dialogue. Buber emphasized the concrete significance of Ḥasidism, placing little value on its abstract ideas. He understood

The *sheva berakhot* (wedding blessings) being recited by three rebbes.

The third president of the State of Israel, Zalman Shazar, had strong Lubavicher sympathies. He is seen here in Kefar Ḥabad celebrating the 19th of Kislev, the anniversary of the release of the first Lubavicher rebbe from prison in Czarist Russia.

the Ḥasidic imperative, "Know Him in all thy ways," as transcending the bounds of the *mitzvot*, as religious experience over and above the *halakhah*.

This view was scathingly attacked by the Zionist Maskil Samuel Joseph ("Shay") Ish-Horowitz (1862-1922), who in *Ha-Ḥasidut ve-ha-Haskalah* (1909) depicted Ḥasidism as a wild, undisciplined movement and the Ba'al Shem Tov as a charlatan. As Horowitz saw it, Ḥasidism contributed no new truths or ways of looking at the world: it simply appropriated to itself the vocabulary of the Kabbalah without fully understanding its implications, and colored it with quasi-philosophical notions "belonging to the household mentality and chronic psychology of the ghetto." The neo-Ḥasidism of Buber attempted to discover in Ḥasidism ethical values and a positive popular force, particularly in the Ḥasidic "joy", which it interpreted as protest against the dejection produced by the conditions of *Galut*; but for Horowitz the Shabbatean movement was to be preferred to Ḥasidism, since it took an upright stand, advocating a breaking free of the bonds of the *Galut* and the ghetto. Horowitz dismissed as arrant nonsense the claims that Ḥasidism was a movement of revival and revolt; far from rebelling against the rabbinate, Ḥasidism retained the *mitzvot* in all their minutiae. He contended that the neo-Ḥasidim were deceiving themselves by interpreting the values of Ḥasidism in secular terms, which he regarded as a perversion of history in the spirit of a new humanism. He believed that Ḥasidism was continuity and not revolt, and that the neo-Ḥasidim did violence to its true nature by depicting it as a revolutionary movement in Jewish history.

A Perversion of History

That Ḥasidism could lend itself to such antithetical interpretations derives from the fact that it represented, in Gershom

The Ponovezher rav, Joseph Kahaneman (died 1969) and the Chryzanover rebbe, David Moses (right). Two hundred years ago the conflict between Mitnaggedim and Ḥasidim was so bitter that it would have been unthinkable for two rabbis from opposing groups to sit together amicably. Although differences remain in the prayers and customs of Ḥasidim and Mitnaggedim, Ḥasidim are now fully accepted and most of the acrimony has gone from the dispute.

Jonathan Twersky of Rotmistrivka (born 1903) on the left, with his son, Velvele Twersky, at the Western Wall in Jerusalem.

Scholem's phrase, "a curious mixture of conservatism and innovation." Its paradoxical attitude towards tradition is nicely illustrated in the reply one ẓaddik gave when he was asked why he did not follow his teacher's example by living as he did. "On the contrary," he said, "I do follow his example, for I have departed from his way just as he departed from that of his teacher."

Essentially Conservative

Despite the charge of its opponents that it set the ẓaddik above the *Shulḥan Arukh*, Ḥasidism in fact never questioned the authority of the Jewish law. Despite the leeway it allowed itself in departing from the *halakhah* in the matter of the time of prayer, it is difficult to avoid the conclusion that Ḥasidism was essentially a conservative movement. Buber himself admitted this

Reb Jekuthiel Judah Halberstam of Klausenburg (second from right) with Levi Eshkol (1895-1969), third prime minister of Israel.

when he said that "the conserving force secretly remained superior to the moving and renewing one and finally conquered it within Ḥasidism itself."

A Struggle Within

One can almost hear Buber sigh as he penned those words. But the statement also highlights the fact that Ḥasidism was not static, that a struggle took place within it to determine the ultimate nature of the movement. Abraham Joshua Heschel has said that Ḥasidism's major revolution was its opposition to what was generally accepted in Judaism – namely, that study is an answer to all problems. And there is no doubt that to a large extent the heresy the early Mitnaggedim detected in Ḥasidism stemmed from the latter's insistence that the study of the Talmud was not the be-all-and-end-all of Judaism.

But quite early in the history of Ḥasidism, its anti-intellectualism ceased to be an article of faith. Although "neo-Ḥasidism" today is applied to Buber's version, historically it might be more accurate to employ the term to Ḥasidism beginning with Shneur Zalman's founding of Ḥabad. For with Ḥabad (which was more than just another "branch" of Ḥasidism) Ḥasidism may be said to have ceased to be exaltation instead of study and to have become exaltation plus study – or even study plus exaltation.

The Message of Ḥasidism

The Hallowing of All Life

So much for the place of Ḥasidism in Jewish history. What of its message? First, the insistence on the hallowing of all life, the consecration of the everyday. Traditional Judaism had always taught that life could not be compartmentalized, that the Jew's

Munkace rebbe, Ḥayyim Eleazar (1871-1937) in the center, with four of his Ḥasidim, strolling in the streets of the spa, Karlsbad. Note the bottles of the mineral water.

religious duties transcended the synagogue and the house of study. In one form or another Jewish teachers down the ages had repeated the rebuke of the prophet Amos: "Yea, though ye offer me burnt-offerings and your meal-offerings, I will not accept them . . . Take thou away from Me the noise of thy songs; and let Me not hear the melody of thy psalteries. But let justice well up as waters, and righteousness as a mighty stream." But Ḥasidism went beyond this when it taught that service of God embraces every aspect of daily life, that there is no place where God does not enter, that there is no human occupation but is an act of worship. "God dwells wherever man lets him in." The doctrine that the most profane action can be done in holiness was not traditional Judaism, and it aroused the particular ire of the Mitnaggedim, who feared that it would lead to the profanation of the holy.

Away with Gloom

Traditional Judaism spoke of "the burden of the *mitzvot*." The obligations of Judaism, in other words, were something that God imposed on the Jew and which the Jew had to fulfill perforce, even though life might be easier without them. But Ḥasidism emphasized the joy of being a Jew. God wants a happy world, and the important thing is to "serve the Lord thy God with joyfulness, and with gladness of heart." Do not live under the weight of sin and guilt. Where there is song and dance, gloom disappears. Do not hesitate to take delight in the world, do not rebel against your desires, but bind these to God.

Ḥasidism, finally lays stress on what God demands of man, of the individual. What can you do as an individual to make earth into heaven? You are unlike any other individual on the face of the earth, and while you cannot change everything you do have responsibility for the piece of world entrusted to you. Rabbi Zusya said just before his death: "In the world to come they will not ask me, 'Why were you not Moses?' They will ask me, 'Why were you not Zusya?' "

"Debate and Study" by Tully Filmus. Tully Filmus is known for his warm realistic sketches of Ḥasidim.

SOURCES

page

3 "Is there no end . . . ? " – quoted in Dinur, *Be-Mifneh ha-Dorot*, p.173.

8 "to preserve those elements of Kabbalism . . ." – Scholem, *Major Trends in Jewish Mysticism*, p.329.

22 "brought Heaven down to earth . . ." – Heschel, *The Earth is the Lord's*, p.75.

24 "his way of tying his shoelaces . . ." – Newman, *The Ḥasidic Anthology*, pp.29f.

25 "When we journeyed to him . . ." – Newman, *The Ḥasidic Anthology*, p.216.

25 "Sin contains repentance . . ." – Newman, *The Ḥasidic Anthology*, p.385.

25 "And before you lie down at night . . ." – Buber, *Tales of the Ḥasidim*, I, p.106.

29 "for this way is dark and bitter . . ." – quoted in Dresner, *The Ẓaddik*, p.51.

31 "There is one mitzvah . . ." – quoted in Dresner, *The Ẓaddik*, p.128. The mitzvah referred to appears in Deuteronomy 10:20.

32 "The outer world . . . " – Schatz-Uffenheimer, in *The Philosophy of Martin Buber*, ed. by Schilpp and Friedman, p. 411.

33 Naḥman of Kossov – Newman, *The Ḥasidic Anthology*, p.343.

33 Levi Isaac of Berdichev – Newman, *The Ḥasidic Anthology*, p.470.

34 Mendel of Kotzk – Buber, *Tales of the Ḥasidim*, II, p.277.

34 "Even in every bodily thing . . ." – quoted in Schilpp and Friedman, eds.. *The Philosophy of Martin Buber*, p.733.

34 "in this lower world . . ." – quoted in Buber, *The Origin and Meaning of Ḥasidism*, p.181.

34 Ḥanokh of Aleksandrow – Buber, *Tales of the Hasidim*, II, p.317.

35 "One eats in consecration . . ." – Buber, *The Origin and Meaning of Ḥasidism*, pp.55f.

36 Ze'ev Wolf of Zhitomir – quoted in Schatz-Uffenheimer, *The Philosophy of Martin Buber*, p.421.

38 "When you are engrossed . . . " – Newman, *The Hasidic Anthology*, p. 327.

38 " . . . a soul and not a clock" – quoted in Rabinowicz, *The World of Ḥasidism*, p.116.

39 "I am in constant fear . . ." – quoted in Dubnow, *Toledot ha-Hasidut*, p.105.

39 "The reason why we should do . . ." – Schechter, "The Chassidim," in *Studies in Judaism*, Meridian paperback, p.175.

41 "When a king is at a celebration . . ." – Newman, *The Ḥasidic Anthology*, p.204.

page

41 "Do you wish to know . . ." – Newman, *The Ḥasidic Anthology*, p.202.

43 "probably the most important legacy . . ." – Scholem, *The Messianic Idea in Judaism*, p.238.

46 "If he who receives *shefa* . . ." – quoted in Dresner, *The Ẓaddik*, p.127.

47 The parable of the king's son – quoted in Dresner, *The Ẓaddik*, p.177.

49 ". . . he too must go down near the slime . . ." – quoted in Ettinger, *Journal of World History*, XI (1–2), (1968), p.258.

49 "Thus Caleb joined . . ." – quoted in Dresner, *The Ẓaddik*, p.178.

49 "The bold-faced go to hell . . ." – Newman, *The Ḥasidic Anthology*, p.295.

53 Jacob Joseph on the ẓaddik's mediation – see Dresner, *The Ẓaddik*, p.279, n.52.

53 "The Lord sometimes likes to show . . ." – Newman, *The Ḥasidic Anthology*, p.260.

54 "the peculiar doctrine of the Intermediary" – Schechter, "The Chassidim," in *Studies in Judaism*, Meridian paperback, p.182.

55 "This simon-pure Ḥasidism . . ." – Scholem, *Major Trends in Jewish Mysticism*, pp.342f.

57 Definition of a Litvak – Samuel, *Prince of the Ghetto*, Meridian paperback, p.192.

60 "I cannot adequately describe . . ." – Mindel, *Rabbi Schneur Zalman*, p.113.

62 "Avigdor the wicked . . ." – Rabinowitsch, *Lithuanian Ḥasidism*, p.61.

67 Anti-Ḥasidic circular in Shklov – Marcus, *The Jew in the Medieval World*, pp.276f.

70 Comparison with Pharisees' opposition to Jesus – Horodezky, *Shivhei ha-Besht*, p.15.

70 A solid basis for the Gaon's fear – quoted in Eliach, *Proceedings of the American Academy for Jewish Research*, v.36 (1968), pp.82f.

77 "men of scholarship, piety and truth" – Mindel, *Rabbi Schneur Zalman*, pp.229f.

78 "We are falsely accused . . ." – quoted in Shapiro, in Jung, *Men of the Spirit*, p.413.

78 Yankel, the tailor – Newman, *The Ḥasidic Anthology*, p.57.

80 ". . . a very scoundrel is better than he" – Buber, *Tales of the Ḥasidim*, II, pp.281f.

81 "one who discards . . ." and "the entire world . . ." – quoted in Mahler, *Ha-Hasidut ve-ha-Haskalah*, p.325.

page

83 "who would stand on the rooftops . . ." – quoted in Mahler, *Ha-Hasidut ve-ha-Haskalah*, p.341.

83 ". . . turned me into water" – quoted in Gutman, *Rabbi Dov mi-Liova*, p. 17.

83 "If he really is a Ḥasid . . ." – quoted in Mahler, *Ha-Hasidut ve-ha-Haskalah*, p.326.

84 "The prohibition against the making of idols . . ." – Newman, *The Ḥasidic Anthology*, p.193.

84 "If I am I . . ." – Buber, *Tales of the Ḥasidim*, II, p.283.

86 ". . . today I took pleasure in your praying" – Buber, *Tales of the Ḥasidim*, II, p.312.

88 "The Rebbe himself never promised . . ." – Zborowski and Herzog, *Life is with People*, pp.172f.

93 ". . . like a pack of famished animals" – Weiner, *9½ Mystics,* p.124.

93 "He who wants to be holy . . ." – quoted in Dresner, *The Ẓaddik*, p.115.

94 "Buber and Belz" – Weiner, *9½ Mystics*, pp.135f.

96 "After all, if we go dressed like this . . ." – quoted in Weiner, *9½ Mystics,* p.187.

96 The dentist who gave up his profession – Mintz, *Legends of the Ḥasidim*, p.57.

97 ". . . a man's world" – Katz, *Tradition and Crisis*, p.243.

100 "If a Ḥasid's motive . . ." – Lipschitz, *The Faith of a Ḥassid*, p.159.

104 Satmarer Ḥasidim harassed Jewish leaders – Gersh and Miller, *Commentary*, Nov. 1959, pp.396f.

105 "S'iz gornisht" – Mintz, *Legends of the Ḥasidim*, p.111.

106 Miracle of the brandy – *Yediot Aḥaronot*, (Tel Aviv), Dec. 21, 1973, p.17 of supplement, "7 Days."

107 "a mission to Jews by Jews" – Lubavitch Foundation of Great Britain, *Challenge*, p.60.

111 "a curious mixture of conservatism and innovation" – Scholem, *Major Trends in Jewish Mysticism*, p.348.

112 "the conserving force secretly remained superior . . ." – Buber, *The Origin and Meaning of Hasidism*, p.127.

READING LIST

Encyclopaedia Judaica, Jerusalem, 1972, under: Dov Baer of Mezhirech, Ḥasidism, Israel ben Eliezer Ba'al Shem Tov, Jacob Isaac of Lublin, Jacob Isaac of Przysucha, Jacob Joseph of Polonnoye, Levi Isaac of Berdichev, Naḥman of Bratslav, Shabbetai Ẓevi, Shneur Zalman of Lyady.

Ben-Amos, Dan, and Mintz, Jerome R., trans. and ed., *In Praise of the Ba'al Shem Tov*, Bloomington, Ind., 1970.

Buber, Martin, *Tales of the Hasidim* 2 vols., New York, 1947–48.

——, *The Origin and Meaning of Hasidism,* Harper Torchbook, New York, 1966.

Dresner, Samuel H., *The Zaddik*, New York, 1960.

Horodezky, Samuel A., *Leaders of Hassidism*, London, 1928.

Langer, Jiri, *Nine Gates*, London, 1961.

Lipschitz, Max A., *The Faith of a Hassid*, New York, 1967.

Levin, Meyer, *The Golden Mountain*, New York, 1951.

Mindel, Nissan, *Rabbi Schneur Zalman*, Brooklyn, N.Y., 1969.

Mintz, Jerome R., *Legends of the Hasidim*, Chicago, 1968.

Rabinowicz, Harry M., *The World of Hasidism,* London, 1970.

Scholem, Gershom, *Major Trends in Jewish Mysticism,* (Ninth Lecture: "Hasidism: The Latest Phase"), New York, 1941.

——, *The Messianic Idea in Judaism,* New York, 1971.

Weiner, Herbert, *9½ Mystics*, New York, 1969.

Wiesel, Elie, *Souls on Fire; Portraits and Legends of Hasidic Masters,* New York, 1972.

ILLUSTRATION CREDITS

Jerusalem, B.M. Ansbacher Collection, p. 2, 16
From Roman Vishniac, *Polish Jews,* New York, 1947, p. 5, 9, 34
Cecil Roth Collection, p. 6, 56, 67
Jerusalem, Sir Isaac and Lady Wolfson Museum in Hechal Shlomo, p. 11
Jerusalem, Gwen Gorr Collection, p. 12
Jerusalem, Jewish National and University Library, p. 14, 26, 40, 63, 66, 87:1, 91
Jerusalem, Shmuel Gorr Photo Collection, p. 18, 43, 48:2, 54:2, 57, 83, 105, 108, 110; color: pl. 5
Tully Filmus, *Selected Drawings* ©Jewish Publication Society of America, Philadelphia, 1971, p. 21, 23, 115
Tel Aviv, Government Press Office, p. 24, 61, 82, 109
Jerusalem, Israel Museum, p. 27, 76:1, 76:2
R. Abramovitch (ed.), *The Vanished World,* New York, 1947, p. 28, 33, 82
Rimon 4 1923, p. 32
Cincinatti, Ohio, Hebrew Union College Museum, p. 37
Photo David Posner, Jerusalem, p. 44,45, 101
Photo K. Weiss, Jerusalem, p.48:1, 51, 74:12, 74:13, 74:14, 74:15, 100, 102, 103, 111, 112
Photo Birnfeld, Tel Aviv, p. 54:1
London, S. Oppenheim, p. 58
M. Balaban, *Historja zydow W Krakowie,* 1936, p. 64
Courtesy Isaac Alfasi, Tel Aviv, p. 74:1, 74:2, 74:7
Courtesy Israel Weinstock, Jerusalem, p. 74:3, 74:4, 74:5, 74:6, 74:8, 74:9, 74:10, 74:11
Photo David Eisenberg, Jerusalem, p. 83
Photo Eden, Jerusalem, G. Drachsler, p. 85
Photo Peter Larsen, Jerusalem, p. 87:2; color: pl. 4 (bottom)
Photo Philip Garvin, from A. Cohen, *A People Apart,* New York, 1970, p. 89
Jerusalem, Leichter Collection, p. 91
Jerusalem, Israel Institute for Sacred Music, p. 95
Photo Zwy Bassey, Jerusalem, p. 98
Jerusalem, Central Archives and Research Institute for the History of Gedolei Israel, p. 106, 113
Mishkan Le-Omanut, Museum of Art, Ein Harod, pl. 1 (top, bottom), pl. 6, pl. 8
Oscar Gruss Collection, New York, pl. 2, pl. 3, pl. 4 (top), pl. 7 (top), cover
Courtesy Dr. and Mrs. I. Goldstein, Jerusalem, pl. 7 (bottom)

Cover: "Ḥasidim in a *Bet Midrash,*" painting by Isidor Kaufmann